*This book is dedicated to the late John-Julian Swanson, OJN,
son of Nashotah House and founder of the
Order of Julian of Norwich*

From Anchorhold to Parish:
English Monasticism & Anglican Spirituality

James Lloyd Breck Conference on Monasticism and the Church
2022

Edited by Greg Peters

Contributions by
Ann Astell
Bryan Spinks

Nashotah House Press

Nashotah House Theological Seminary
2777 Mission Road
Nashotah, WI 53058

Religion

ISBN-13 978-0-9792243-8-6

From Anchorhold to Parish: English Monasticism & Anglican Spirituality

JAMES LLOYD BRECK CONFERENCE
ON
MONASTICISM AND THE CHURCH
2022

Edited by
Greg Peters

Acknowledgments

The Breck Conference would not be possible without the support of Dr. Garwood Anderson, Dean, and the residential faculty of Nashotah House.

The staff of Nashotah House, especially Jim Watkins, Cam Walker, Kelly Medina, and Randy Savage also provided invaluable service.

Dawn Anderson and the Rev. Ben Jefferies helped prepare the talks for publication.

Without the generous endowment of the Order of St. Benedict Servants of Christ, there would be no James Lloyd Breck Conference on Monasticism and the Church.

Introduction

The James Lloyd Breck Conference on Monasticism and the Church is made possible by a generous endowment granted to Nashotah House Theological Seminary in 2017, extending the legacy of the Order of St. Benedict Servants of Christ into perpetuity for the advancement of Religious Life, especially within Anglicanism. Founded in 1968 by the Very Rev. Dom Cornelis deRijk, OSB (along with the Rev. Canon Lewis Long), in Phoenix, Arizona, the Order was a Benedictine community guided by the balance of prayer, study, and work. Rev. deRijk, the last prior of the Order, received his Master of Divinity degree from Nashotah House in 1976. With his passing in 2016 the Order closed, but its end allows for a new beginning with the creation of the annual Breck Conference.

The conference name was chosen to honor one of the founders of Nashotah House while also being clear that the conference was on monasticism but with the purpose of recovering elements of the Christian monastic tradition for the contemporary church. James Lloyd Breck, while a student at General Theological Seminary in New York, responded to an invitation by Bp. Jackson Kemper to come to the Wisconsin frontier. In correspondence with his brother, Breck wrote, "The following is mooted [i.e., spoken] in our class–and be not surprised if time should strengthen it–that six or eight of us clan together, going out West, place ourselves under Bishop Kemper, all at one point, and there educate and preach; to live under one roof, constituted into a Religious House, under a Superior."[1] Simply put, Breck imagined that what was to become Nashotah House was a monastic endeavor.[2]

The theme of the third conference, held on the campus of Nashotah House from June 23-25, 2022, was "From Anchorhold to Parish: English Monasticism & Anglican Spirituality." The sixteenth-century Church of England was greatly influenced by late medieval English monastic spirituality. John Bede Pauley and Bede Thomas Mudge have both shown the monastic influence, especially from the Benedictines, on the Book of Common Prayer; and scholars such as Eamon Duffy have demonstrated the continuity between late medieval devotional practices and early Anglican piety. The use of the vernacular and an emphasis on the suffering Jesus, for example, are late medieval themes that recur in early Anglican faith and practice. Thus, the 2022 conference sought to explicate how late medieval English monastic spirituality was resourced by

---

[1] James Lloyd Breck, June 15, 1840, letter to his brother Charles; cited in *The Life of the Reverend James Lloyd Breck, D.D., chiefly from Letters Written by Himself*, compiled by Charles Breck (New York: E. & J. B. Young & Co., 1883), 8.

[2] Thomas C. Reeves, "James Lloyd Breck and the Founding of Nashotah House," *Anglican and Episcopal History* 65.1 (1996), 56: "James Lloyd Breck was the most zealous member of the quartet, and the one most interested in monasticism."

early Anglican Christians in both their personal devotional life and in parish practice.

The conference consisted of four plenary talks by two speakers and included much time for informal discussion and interaction. The speakers included

Dr. Ann W. Astell (Professor of Theology at the University of Notre Dame)

Rev. Dr. Bryan D. Spinks (Bishop F. Percy Goddard Professor Emeritus of Liturgical Studies and Pastoral Theology at Yale Divinity School)

The "Mixed Life" Of Late Medieval English Monasticism

Dr. Ann W. Astell

THE ESTATES SATIRE of Chaucer's *Canterbury Tales* and Langland's *Piers Plowman* foregrounds individual portraits of imperfect monks, friars, and nuns against the background of a high religious ideal.[1] In the fourteenth and fifteenth centuries, monastic life in England was quite different from that during the piously remembered, earlier ages of Cuthbert (634– 687), Bede (c. 672–735), Anselm of Canterbury (c.1033–1109), and Aelred of Rievaulx (1110–1167). But how is that historical difference to be assessed? Setting aside the cases of obvious abuse, one wonders: how we are to judge the monks and nuns of this period, and what we might learn from them? Were late medieval monks and nuns living worldly lives, as measured by the ancient rule, or mixed lives, appropriate to then-current mitigated rules and responsive to the Holy Spirit's guidance in altered social conditions?

---

[1] Geoffrey Chaucer, *The Canterbury Tales*, in *The Riverside Chaucer*, ed. Larry D. Benson, 3rd ed. (Boston: Houghton Mifflin, 1987); William Langland, *The Vision of Piers Plowman: A Complete Edition of the B-Text*, ed. A. V. C. Schmidt (New York: E. P. Dutton, 1978).

The expression "mixed life" is traditionally used as a technical term in spirituality studies to describe a way of holiness that is partly active, partly contemplative—a combination of the busyness of Martha with the attentive stillness of her sister Mary or (to use another biblical figure) a combination of the fertility of Leah in good works with the ardent languishing of Rachel for spiritual union with God.[2] Monastic life was always mixed to some extent in its combination of work (the *opus Dei* of the Divine Office) and prayer, in its recognition of different spiritual stages (carnal, rational, spiritual) among its members,[3] and (to a greater or lesser extent) in its division of labor. The early, self-sustaining Cistercians, for example, had monks who worked in husbandry, as cooks, as physicians in the infirmaries, as farmers in the fields, as carpenters and masons, as tailors, teachers, and scribes.[4]

---

[2] On the tradition of the two lives, see Cuthbert Butler, *Western Mysticism, with Afterthoughts*, 2nd ed. (London: Constable and Company, 1926), 157–88, 191–98.

[3] On these three stages, which correspond to a tripartite theological anthropology, see William of St. Thierry, *The Golden Epistle: A Letter to the Brethren at Mont Dieu*, trans. Theodore Berkeley, OCSO (Kalamazoo, MI: Cistercian Publications, 1971).

[4] For a twentieth-century description of life at the Trappist monastery in Gethsemane, Kentucky, see Thomas Merton, *The Seven-Storey Mountain: An Autobiography of Faith* ([1948] Boston: Houghton Mifflin Harcourt, 1998). Trappist monks are Cistercians of the Strict Observance. Merton describes their way of life as "active contemplation" (428). He discusses the contemplative life of the monks as a "mixed life," echoing Thomas Aquinas and extending his analysis of three states of life: active, contemplative, and mixed (453–58). According to Merton, "The fact is, there does not exist any such thing as a purely contemplative Order of men—an Order which does not have, somewhere in its constitution, the note of *contemplata tradere* [that is, the obligation to pass on to others what one has received in contemplative union with God]" (456).

The term "mixed life," however, is seldom applied to the monastic way, which is conceived to be purely contemplative in its goal, in contrast to the goals of the "active life" of the laity and of the "mixed life" of the mendicants. Used in this lecture, it fittingly describes creative polarities within late medieval English monasticism itself in an age of confraternities,[5] parish and trade guilds,[6] almoner schools,[7] colleges,[8] and universities—all of them contributing to what Gail McMurray Gibson calls the "hybrid blend of monastic and lay spirituality that is such a signature of fifteenth-century Suffolk and Norfolk culture."[9] This blend, I argue, precipitated a kind of identity-crisis for the monks and nuns themselves as they struggled to continue and to adjust their contemplative way of life in changed times; it made them vulnerable both to deserved criticism and to undeserved attack; it also suited them, however, to a devout laity that consciously aspired to the "mixed life" and thus

[5] See Karen Stöber, "Manifestations of Monastic Patronage in the Later Middle Ages," in *Late Medieval Monasteries and Their Patrons: England and Wales, c.1300–1540* (Woodbridge, Suffolk, UK: Boydell Press, 2007), 65–111.

[6] See Eamon Duffy, *The Stripping of the Altars: Traditional Religion in England, 1400–1580*, 2nd ed. (New Haven: Yale University Press, 1992).

[7] See James G. Clark, "Monasteries and Secular Education in Late Medieval England," in *Monasteries and Society in the British Isles in the Later Middle Ages,* ed. Janet Burton and Karen Stöber (Woodbridge, Suffolk, UK: Boydell Press, 2008), 145–67.

[8] See Martin Heale, "Colleges and Monasteries in Late Medieval England," *The Late Medieval English College and Its Context,* ed. Clive Burgess and Martin Heale (Woodbridge, Suffolk, UK: York Medieval Press, 2008), 67–86.

[9] Gail McMurray Gibson, *The Theater of Devotion: East Anglian Drama and Society in Late Medieval England* (Chicago: University of Chicago Press, 1989), 127.

made them, in confraternity with the laity, forerunners in the end for a "monasticized" Church in the land marked by their historical ruins.

Traditionally identified by themselves and others as contemplatives, the monks and nuns of late medieval England—not unlike the devout laity with whom they increasingly associated—found themselves to be living, in fact, a mixed life of action and contemplation, although the precise mix and forms of each varied from person to person and across the religious landscape. Studies of lay piety and vernacular theology in England show that the laity were conscious of their call to holiness and that many also aspired to Christian perfection in a mixed life inclusive of good works, meditation, and (at its peak) contemplation.[10] What has been less often noticed is the degree to which men and women in the monasteries ardently fostered this very aspiration in their lay friends and benefactors; perceiving it alive in others, they also drew inspiration from it for a monasticism renewed at its root.

In this first lecture I focus on the older monastic orders, the Benedictines, and the Augustinian canons—the orders most affected in England by trends away from lives of strict, solitary enclosure. I proceed in four steps: first, to recall the larger historical picture; second, to comment upon monk-authored Latin treatises from the period written in defense of monasticism; third, to examine the "mixed life" itself as presented in vernacular writings by monks addressed to

---

[10] See Hilary M. Carey, "Devout Literate Laypeople and the Pursuit of the Mixed Life in Later Medieval England," *Journal of Religious History* (Jan. 1, 1987): 361–81; Eamon Duffy, *Marking the Hours: English People & Their Prayers, 1240–1570* (New Haven, CT: Yale University Press, 2006).

lay audiences; fourth, to suggest that monks writing and reading these same vernacular works began to see in them a mirror for their own more "active" reform, a mirror not far removed from that controversially sketched out for them by Bishop Reginald Pecock in his *Reule of Crysten Religeoun* (1443–1449).

The Historical Context

According to James Clark, the fifteenth century witnessed a resurgence of the religious orders in England: "in 1500 there were . . . no fewer than 900 religious communities in England and Wales, including 28 that had been established since 1350. . . . By most estimates, there were probably about 6500 monks, friars, and nuns living in England and Wales in 1400. By 1500 this number had increased to more than 9000, an especially significant increase since the overall population level remained stagnant."[11] Given first this trajectory of growth; second, the long tradition of royal endowments recently renewed by Henry V (1387–1422) through two new monastic foundations at Sheen and Syon; and third, the multiple legal protections for religious houses, the Dissolution in the 1530s came as a shock and a scandal.[12]

That said, it remains nonetheless true that the years between the Black Death (1346 to 1353) and the

---

[11] James G. Clark, "The Religious Orders in Pre-Reformation England," in *The Religious Orders in Pre-Reformation England,* ed. James G. Clark (Woodbridge, Suffolk, UK: Boydell Press, 2002), 3–33, at 7.

[12] Peter Cunich, "The Ex-Religious in Post-Dissolution Society: Symptoms of Post-Traumatic Stress Disorder?" in *Religious Orders in Pre-Reformation England,* 227–38, at 233.

Dissolution were anxious years for the people of England and for members of religious houses in particular. The world, as more than one poet described it, was unstable. Like the surrounding towns, the monasteries had lost between a third and a half of their members during the pandemic—a human loss with economic consequences, giving rise to laborers' revolts, notably the 1381 rising in London, St. Albans, and Bury St. Edmunds. Many smaller religious houses—especially those of the Augustinian canons—had had to close. The Hundred Years' War between England and France (1337-1453)—a war opposed by the Benedictines and by all religious houses in England with ties to the continent—led to their increased taxation and to the suppression of alien priories.[13] Returning from France, Henry V, in an unprecedented move, assembled over 350 Black Friars (monks and prelates) in Westminster in 1421 and called them to reform in thirteen articles.[14]

The Great Schism (1378 to 1417) in the Church between rival papacies in Rome, Avignon, and Pisa further unsettled religious life in England during the war years, as did the rise of Lollardy. In 1410, the Lollards formally petitioned Parliament for the disendowment of the monasteries and the redistribution of their wealth—a prospect that was appealing to some already powerful, greedy lords until the Oldcastle Revolt of 1414 linked Lollardy with treason

---

[13] Dom David Knowles, *The Religious Orders in England*, 3 vols. (Cambridge, England: Cambridge University Press, 1948, 1955, 1959), 2:157–66.

[14] Knowles, *The Religious Orders in England*, 2:182–84.

against the king. The trials against heretics under Thomas Arundel (1353–1414), Archbishop of Canterbury and Lord Chancellor of England, enabled the episcopacy to exert juridical authority over territories belonging to the monasteries, undermining abbatial authority.

As the war between England and France came to its close, civil war shortly ensued in England during the interrupted reigns of Henry VI (1421–1471). The War of the Roses (1455–1485) between Lancastrian and Yorkist claimants to the English throne complicated the relationship between monasteries in the north and south of England and their individual relationships to the crown; Tewkesbury Abbey became, in fact, a bloody battle site and needed to be re-consecrated.

These external factors combined with others to effect a series of changes in the inner life of the older monastic orders in England: Benedictine, Augustinian, and Cistercian. Most notably, perhaps, the canons *Summi magistri* issued by Pope Benedict XII in 1336 required not only an annual Chapter to be held within every monastery but also a triennial General Chapter of the two provinces of the Black Monks, north and south, to be presided over by an elected abbot, in order to regulate monastic practices more uniformly by statute. The papal canons further directed that a certain percentage of Benedictine monks (one out of every twenty) be sent to the universities for study and that young monks be taught grammar, logic, and philosophy in the cloister. Accepting then-current mitigations of the Rule, Benedict XII made allowance for half of the monks to eat meat on given days (Sunday, Monday, Tuesday, and Thursday), excluding the seasons of Advent and Lent (Septuagesima to Easter),[15] but he reprobated the widely accepted (and perduring) wage-system, by which individual monks received a monetary allowance (*peculium*) for the purchase of personal items (clothes, medicinal spice) and for recreation, for example, during home visits to family members.[16] In *Ad decorum*, issued by the same pope in 1339, similar decrees concerning education, ascetical practice, and governance were issued for the Augustinian canons, whose Rule was always more lenient than the Rule of St. Benedict.[17]

Other changes, coming from without and from within, also affected the common life. The frequent granting of papal chaplaincies, especially to Austin canons, and the permission given to canons to hold benefices "cut at the roots of religious life," David Knowles observes, by exempting the chaplains from regular life and encouraging their individual pursuits of clerical careers.[18] Pressed with administrative work and duties at Parliament, late medieval abbots kept separate apartments and frequently dined with guests, rather than with the other monks under their fatherly charge, and this privilege of personal living

---

[15] Knowles, *The Religious Orders in England*, 2:1–5.

[16] Knowles, *The Religious Orders in England*, 2:5, 184, 241–42.

[17] Knowles, *The Religious Orders in England*, 2:7.

[18] Knowles, *The Religious Orders in England*, 2:171.

space was extended to others.[19] Benedictine monasteries rented or leased their properties—a move that increased the interaction between monks and laity, secularized the monastic landscape, and led to a higher percentage of monks functioning as obedientiaries, that is, as administrators exempt by office from regular participation in the common life of the refectory and choir.[20] Chaucer's satirized Monk en route to Canterbury is one of these obedientiaries, "a kepere of the celle," "an outridere," whose exemptions have had the effect of instilling in him a disdain for the supposedly outmoded "reule of Seint Maure or of Seint Beneit" (GP 172, 166, 173).[21]

Riding on horseback out to oversee the monastery's holdings, the Monk has also distanced himself from occupations traditionally belonging to monks: psalmody, the reading and studying of books, and the writing and copying of manuscripts:[22] "What sholde he studie and make hymselven wood, / Upon a book in cloystre alwey to poure [?]" (GP 184–85). Although the monasteries continued to operate scriptoria, these workplaces increasingly vied for commissions with scriptoria in urban centers outside the monasteries—a rise in production made possible by higher levels of literacy among the laity, increased documentary

---

[19] Knowles, *The Religious Orders in England*, 3:461; 2:244–45.

[20] Knowles, *The Religious Orders in England*, 2:240, 309, 328.

[21] *The Riverside Chaucer*, ed. Larry D. Benson, 3rd ed. (Boston: Houghton Mifflin, 1987). I quote from the General Prologue (GP) of *The Canterbury Tales*.

[22] Knowles, *The Religious Orders in England*, 2:234–35.

demands by a growing bureaucracy, and a flourishing book trade. In the later fifteenth century, three Benedictine monasteries—Abingdon, St. Albans, and Tavistock—did introduce their own printing presses, playing what James Clark calls "an important role in the development of printing in the decades before the Dissolution,"[23] but the new technologies also necessarily altered the meditative, communal relationship between the monks and their work.[24]

The troubled two centuries before the Dissolution are treated in the second volume of Dom David Knowles's magisterial work, *The Religious Orders in England*—a volume he entitles "The End of the Middle Ages."[25] As Joan Greatrex observes, Knowles's monumental history "remains a *sine qua non* for all students in the field because many of his conclusions still stand, even though they were by-and-large based on the printed sources then available to him."[26] The clear-eyed picture that Knowles paints of the monks and their monasteries does not gloss over individual and institutional failings, but it shows them to have arisen in the context of manifold social, cultural, and political changes, amidst which religious people, men and women alike, strove to live according to their respective rules, albeit in

---

[23] Clark, "The Religious Orders in Pre-Reformation England," 24.

[24] Knowles, *The Religious Orders in England*, 3:461–62.

[25] The three volumes of Knowles's history, cited above, were published in 1948, 1955, and 1959, respectively.

[26] Joan Greatrex, "After Knowles: Recent Perspectives in Monastic History," in *The Religious Orders in Pre-Reformation England*, 35–47, at 35.

conditions burdened with rich legacies difficult to maintain and quite different from those that had existed at the time and place of their foundations.

The wealth of more recent historical scholarship that draws upon manuscript sources largely corroborates Knowles's conclusions but tends in the direction of a rosier assessment of English monasticism—a monasticism seen to be undergoing its own reformation from within, but still unsure about the direction that reform should take and in search of models. Should reform take the route of a smaller, more strictly enclosed, contemplative monasticism—the route exemplified by the Carthusians and the Bridgettines at Syon? Or should monastic reform accentuate the educational tradition and famous hospitality of the Benedictine monasteries through new engagements with a laity hungry for spiritual reading, spiritual direction, and pilgrimage to holy places? "Even the wisest of saints," Knowles observes, "have been unable to decide when the duty of preserving a precious heritage takes precedence over the duty of offering a spiritual treasure freely to all."[27]

---

[27] Knowles, *The Religious Orders in England*, 3:461.

Studies in Monastic Origins:
The English Apologiae for Monasticism

The way forward wisely entails a looking back to first principles, to the original type of a thing. As the religious landscape of medieval England became more variegated through the introduction there of the Franciscans and the Dominicans, an unnamed Black Friar at Bury St. Edmunds wrote an original treatise on monastic origins and spirituality for Hugh de Chiverey, abbot of Tournus in Burgurdy (1361–1367). It was widely circulated in England and partly plagiarized—with timely additions, revisions, and extractions—over the course of the following century and a half by leading monks at Bury (among them, the bibliographer John Boston, fl. 1410, and the hostillar Andrew Aston, c.1426), at Durham (by Richard of Segbroke, c. 1390; Uthred of Boldon, d. 1397; and John Wessyngton, c. 1440), at St. Albans (by Thomas Walsingham, c. 1390, and John Whethamstede, c.1440), at Glastonbury (by John Merylynch, 1402–20), and at Christ Church, Canterbury (by William Gillingham, 1367–1409). Comparing and contrasting the successive iterations, William Patin discerns various motives for the composition of these treatises—antiquarian interest, personal devotion, the desire to raise an in-house call for reform or to register an *ad extra* defense of monasticism against mendicant and Lollard critiques by presenting it as theologically justified and as contributing to the common good of society.[28] The *apologiae* continued to be read and copied up until the Dissolution. Knowles calls Uthred of Boldon's rendition "an extremely reasonable, persuasive, and historically accurate account of the development of the monastic ideal."[29] Pantin draws the summary conclusion: "These treatises reveal the older monasticism as consciously on the defensive [already] in the fourteenth century."[30]

Since these Latin treatises have never been fully transcribed from the surviving manuscripts nor translated, and because they give a rare look at what the late medieval monks thought about their own way of life, a summary at least of the earliest, fourteenth-century treatise on the topic is warranted here, following Pantin's description of it.

Composed in four parts, the treatise begins with a section in twelve chapters on monastic origins. Citing evidence in Gregory the Great's *Dialogues*, the Life of Saint Augustine, and a sermon by Odo of Cluny (d. 942), the writer begins in chapter one by acknowledging that the earliest monastic communities predate that founded by Benedict of Nursia (480–548) in the sixth century. Citing authorities such as John Chrysostom, John Cassian, Jerome, and Josephus, he then turns to Sacred Scripture in Chapters two through four, finding monks in the Old Testament (e.g., Samuel, the

---

[28] W. A. Pantin, "Some Medieval English Treatises on the Origins of Monasticism," in *Medieval Studies Presented to Rose Graham*, ed. Veronica Ruffer and A.J. Taylor (Oxford: Oxford University Press, 1950), 189–215, esp. 202–05.

[29] Knowles, *The Religious Orders in England*, 2:52.

[30] Pantin, "Some Medieval English Treatises on the Origins of Monasticism," 210; see also Knowles, *The Religious Orders in England*, 2:270–72.

Sons of the Prophets, Elias, Eliseus, and the Rechabites);
among the Essenes; and in the New Testament. There John
the Baptist, fasting and preaching in the desert, appears
as a primary example, but also Saint Peter, who gave up
everything to follow Christ (Matt. 19:27), and the Christian
communities after Pentecost: "They devoted themselves to
the teaching of the apostles and to the communal life, to the
breaking of bread and to the prayers" (Acts 2:42). Above
all, the writer points to Christ himself as the true author of
all monasticism. Tempted in the wilderness, Jesus declares
his single-hearted monotheism: "The Lord, your God, shall
you worship, and him alone shall you serve" (Matt. 4:10; Dt
6:4, 13); to his disciples, Jesus enjoins the renunciation of
earthly goods (Matt. 19:21) and the taking up of the cross
(Luke 9:23).

Chapters five and six discuss the rule of the cenobites
at the time of the apostles (Acts 4:34) and in Egypt after
their time, recalling descriptions of the Alexandrian
monks by Eusebius and Philo Judaeus and those of the
Egyptian monks given by Jerome and Cassian concerning
governance, psalmody, poverty, economy, and food.
Chapter eight explains the monk's tonsure and crown.
Chapter nine, devoted to the Rule of St. Benedict and
responding to the Joachite theology of history,[31] contains
the remarkable claim that "while the *ordo coniugatorum*
[order of the married] has the image of the Father, and the

---

[31] See Morton W. Bloomfield and Marjorie E. Reeves, "The Penetration of
Joachism into Northern Europe," *Speculum* 29.4 (1954): 772–93.

ordo clericorum [order of the clergy] the image of the Son, the *ordo coenobitarum* [order of the cenobites, that is, of monks living in community] has the image of the Holy Ghost," and that, as a charismatic force in history, it has given rise to cenobites in every age: "before the law, under the law, and under the Gospel."[32] Monasticism thus appears not as an outdated institution within the Church but as a constant, ever renewed, movement of evangelical witness and reform.

In keeping with its exaltation of the common life, chapter ten treats anchorites and hermits as "the flower" of the cenobitic way, noting that some cenobites "pass on" to the eremitical state.[33] The author contrasts true cenobites and hermits with the fraudulent Sarabaites (treated in chapter eleven)—hypocrites so-called after Ananias and Saphira (Acts 5:1–11)—and the wandering Gyrovagi, lacking in stability, who take the world for their cloister (discussed in chapter twelve).

Following this first part of his apologia, the monk of Bury celebrates and defends monasticism in a second part, wherein he gives the names of 210 monastic saints, cited from various sources (among them Gregory's *Dialogues*; the *Vita patrum*; Cassiodorus's *Historia tripartita*; Isidore of Seville's *De viris illustribus*; and the *Legenda Aurea*), and he leaves room at the end of his list for the addition of more

---

[32] Pantin, "Some Medieval English Treatises on the Origins of Monasticism," 191.

[33] Pantin, "Some Medieval English Treatises on the Origins of Monasticism," 191.

entries.[34] A third part describes twelve non-Benedictine monastic Orders, arranged in chronological sequence by the dates of their foundation, whose members live according to the rule given them by their respective founders.[35] The list contains orders still familiar to us: the Augustinian canons, Carthusians, Cistercians, Praemonstratensians, Dominicans, Franciscans, Austin Friars, and Carmelites, but also orders since extinct: the military orders of the Templars and the Hospitallers; the Order of Grandmont; the Order of the Brothers of Vallis Scolarium;[36] and the once flourishing Order of Sempringham, founded in England circa 1148 by a parish priest named Gilbert.

In the context of the treatise as a whole, this listing of the religious orders enfolds them all within a single, developing monastic tradition, rooted in Christ himself and moved by the Holy Spirit. The list notably includes Orders that claimed for themselves a mixed life of contemplation and action as preachers, missionaries, teachers, pastors, and soldiers. The Dominicans had adopted with modifications the monastic Rule of St. Augustine, and the Rule of the Templars was derived from the Rule of St. Benedict, as interpreted and adapted for them by Bernard of Clairvaux (1090–1153). Emphasizing their family resemblance and

---

[34] Pantin, "Some Medieval English Treatises on the Origins of Monasticism," 192.

[35] Pantin, "Some Medieval English Treatises on the Origins of Monasticism," 192–94.

[36] On this order, see Richard W. Emery, "The Friars of the Blessed Mary and the Pied Friars," *Speculum* 24.2 (1949): 228–38.

historical interconnections, the Benedictine writer suggests that the older monastic orders looked upon the more recently founded orders as offspring of, and genial competitors with, themselves—offspring who set a challenge and a mirror for their own renewal, to the extent that they could do so without losing their own essential identities and traditions, such as *stabilitas loci* [stability of place].

A fourth and final part of the work thus strikes an explicitly apologetic note, defending the older monasteries as "possessioners" against the Franciscans' view of apostolic poverty. Commending the wisdom of those who practice holy poverty through the communal possession of goods, the Benedictine writer cites the example of the apostles who held all things in common (Acts 4:32) and were therefore able to extirpate cupidity, to cultivate humility, to attain to the tranquility of heart necessary for contemplation, and, free from concern about carnal things, to focus instead on heavenly wisdom.[37]

The monk of Bury's treatise just described is scholastic in its encyclopedic interest, its sense of history, and its argumentative presentation of reasons in support of monastic endowment. The treatise does not cite Thomas Aquinas's defense of common possession and of the mixed life in the *Summa theologica*, and there is no indication that the monk knew that work directly, but the treatise evinces a definite awareness of the questions being debated in the

---

[37] Pantin, "Some Medieval English Treatises on the Origins of Monasticism," 212–13.

schools about the religious orders. Against the monk of Bury's implicit claim that there is really only one religious order—that of the monks—Thomas argues that although all the Orders enjoin vows of poverty, chastity, and obedience and strive for Christian perfection in charity, the different Orders can be distinguished from each other both through the particular works of charity to which they are directed and through their respective ascetical practices.[38]

Departing from the idea of a single, contemplative root, Thomas argues further that an Order may be established for works of the active life, in particular, the corporal works of mercy praised by Jesus in Matthew 25:35-40—works that are sacrificial services offered both visibly to one's neighbor and, in a hidden way, to God.[39] Building upon that conclusion, Thomas defends the possibility of Orders established for the spiritual works of mercy—teaching, preaching, administering the sacraments.[40] Since the performance of these works requires study, Thomas considers how and why the ascetical practice of study belongs both to the contemplative and to the mendicant orders, indeed to all the religious orders.[41]

Final in this logical sequence, Thomas asks the question of the relative excellence of the contemplative and active orders. The Dominican Master grants the superiority

---

[38] Thomas Aquinas, *Summa theologica*, Pars II-II, Q 188, art 1.

[39] Thomas Aquinas, *Summa theologica*, Pars II-II, Q 188, art 2.

[40] Thomas Aquinas, *Summa theologica*, Pars II-II, Q 188, art. 4.

[41] Thomas Aquinas, *Summa theologica*, Pars II-II, Q 188, art. 5.

THE "MIXED LIFE" OF ENGLISH MONASTICISM 23

of the contemplative life over that of an active life devoted exclusively to the corporal works of mercy, but he troubles the claim of the contemplatives to the greatest excellence (given their singular, charitable focus on God, the Highest Good) by referring to those orders directed toward the spiritual works of mercy. Since these works of teaching and preaching, like the works of contemplation, require biblical reading and theological study and are perfectly accomplished as an overflow of contemplative union with God, they are best understood as the proper end of a mixed life of contemplation and action. Thomas maintains, "And this work is more excellent than simple contemplation. For even as it is better to enlighten than merely to shine, so it is better to give to others the fruits of one's contemplation than merely to contemplate."[42]

Thomas's high theology of the mixed life appealed both to the English laity and to late medieval monks and nuns who were increasingly living a mixed life rather than a purely contemplative life and who were doing so consciously. Somewhat contrary to his own intentions to distinguish the active mendicants from the contemplative monastics, Thomas's arguments in the *Summa* include, in fact, many quotations from Cassian's *Conferences* that, taken in their original context, support a "mixed" view of monastic life. Thomas concludes his *respondeo* to Article Two of Question 188 with a brief paraphrase of the teaching of Abbot Nesteros in *Conferences* 14.4, using it to exemplify

---

[42] Thomas Aquinas, *Summa theologica*, Pars II-II, Q 188, art. 6.

the different aims of the various religious orders. The full text, however, first defines *Praktike* (πρακτική) as a practiced knowledge of vice to be avoided and virtue to be pursued; it then indicates that this two-fold knowledge is obtained through active participation in various good works, which Nesteros illustrates through a number of desert fathers, all of them contemplatives: Abba John, "who presided over a large cenobium near the town called Thmuis;" Abba Macarius, gentle in spirit, who "presided over a hostel in Alexandria," and who "should not be considered inferior to any of those who pursued the remoteness of the desert."[43] Others, Nesteros observes, "choose the care of the sick, others carry out the intercession that is owed to the downtrodden and the oppressed, some are intent upon teaching, and others give alms to the poor."[44] The ascent up the rungs of the contemplative ladder is clearly grounded in practical action at the base, but that ascent makes possible, in turn, a descent in charity to that same base.

Vernacular Theologies of the Mixed Life: The Monastic Contributions

Thomas's teaching on the mixed life was certainly known to Walter Hilton (c. 1340–1396). Hilton cites Thomas by

---

[43] John Cassian, *The Conferences*, trans. Boniface Ramsey, O.P., Ancient Christian Writers 57 (New York: Paulist Press, 1997), 506–07.

[44] Ibid., 507.

name in his letter to his friend Adam Horsley, a clerk in the Exchequer who was about to enter the Carthusian Order. In this letter "On the Usefulness and Prerogatives of Religion" (*De Utilitate et Prerogativis Religionis*), Hilton commends Horsley's decision and reveals that he himself is considering religious life. Fulfilling that intention as an Augustinian canon, Hilton went on to write a number of important spiritual texts, the most famous of these being the *Ladder of Perfection* (*Scala Perfectionis*), first printed by Wynkyn de Worde in 1494, and *The Mixed Life*, an epistolary treatise in Middle English, printed in 1506 by Richard Pynson with the title "To a Devout Man in Temporal Estate."

This last-mentioned text interests us here. Written by a monk to a layman aspiring to Christian perfection, Hilton's *Mixed Life* first explains that there are two states of life in which Christians can please God and attain to Heaven's bliss: "þat oon is bodili, and þat oþir is goostli."[45] Hilton explains to his "dere broþir in Crist" that the "bodili" or carnal state principally pertains to men and women at work in the world, but that it also pertains to novices in religious life, who must first break down the unruliness of the body through reason and discipline, in order to render it flexible and ready for spiritual works: "Bodili wirchynge gooþ bifore, and goostli comeþ aftir."[46] When sinful habits have been overcome, however, bodily work continues, taking

[45] *Walter Hilton's "Mixed Life" Edited from Lambeth Palace MS 472*, ed. S. J. Ogilvie-Thomson (Salzburg: Institut für Anglistik und Amerikanistik, Universität Salzburg, 1986), 1, line 3.

[46] *Walter Hilton's "Mixed Life"* 1, line 1; 2, line 14.

various forms: the penitential practices of self-denial (e.g., fasting, vigils); the charitable works of mercy, corporal and spiritual; and the bearing of physical illness for the sake of righteousness. Clearly these bodily works also apply both to the laity and to religious who are no longer novices.

Like Thomas, who stresses the goal of perfect charity, Hilton counsels his friend to proceed according to the order of charity, fulfilling his earthly duties to his children and to all those in his charge, performing the works of the active life and intermingling them with spiritual works of the contemplative life ("wiþ goostli werkes of lif contemplatif"), such as prayers, meditations, and the reading of Sacred Scripture.[47] This combination constitutes a third manner of living, Hilton explains, which adds the savor of love and devotion—indeed, the fervor of love—to the doing of good works.[48] This mixed life is lived by prelates and other curates as well as by devout laypeople who bear responsibility for others, e.g., spouses, children, servants, tenants. Hilton goes on to present Jesus himself as the example par excellence of someone living the mixed life.[49] Later he proposes to his friend the example of Jacob, who won for himself two wives, Leah and Rachel, and thereby merited the name "Israel," becoming a true contemplative, a man seeing God, imperfectly in this earthly life, perfectly in Heaven.[50]

---

[47] *Walter Hilton's "Mixed Life"* 10, line 102.

[48] *Walter Hilton's "Mixed Life"* 11–12, lines 117–121.

[49] *Walter Hilton's "Mixed Life"* 17–18, lines 177–195.

[50] *Walter Hilton's "Mixed Life"* 28–33, lines 311–378.

Hilton counsels persons with a markedly contemplative vocation, however, to hold fast to the works of prayer and to avoid engaging themselves in active works, except in cases of great need for the relief of others in body and soul or at the bidding of their religious superior and, in every case, for a limited time.[51] Whether living an active, a mixed, or a contemplative life, the key to charity's perfection, Hilton advises, is the constant fostering of the heart's desire for God: "þe more desire þat þou hast to him and for him, þe more is þe fier of loue in þee" [the greater the desire that you have toward him and for him, the greater is the fire of love in thee].[52]

The counsel the Augustinian monk then proceeds to give to his lay friend about meditative prayer exercises clearly reflects Hilton's own experiences in prayer. While the Augustinian monk sees the higher level of contemplation as largely attainable only by religious at a certain peak of the monastic life, he makes it clear both in *The Mixed Life* and in *Ladder of Perfection* that the lower tier of the contemplative life—that of meditation—is open both to lay people and to monks, who are vowed to practice it.

The *imitatio monastici* (imitation of the monastic way) that Hilton proposes to his brother in Christ is one that Anne Clark Bartlett describes as "highly attractive to late medieval English laypeople," as evidenced by the "increasing installation of private chapels in noble households;" the

---

[51] *Walter Hilton's "Mixed Life"* 21–22, lines 227–237.

[52] *Walter Hilton's "Mixed Life"* 40, lines 464–465.

proliferation of written portraits of pious laypersons, such as Cecily, Duchess of York, who practiced quasi-monastic disciplines; and "the burgeoning coteries of literate laity who gathered around monastic houses."[53] Monastic poets like John Lydgate (1370–c.1451), the famous monk of Bury, and John Audelay (died c. 1426),[54] who resided in his last years with Augustinian canons at Haughmond Abbey, translated Latin liturgical works into English poetry, often in alternating forms that employed both languages.[55] Thus they aimed not only at the full participation of the laity in the liturgy, but also at the visible conjoining of the monastic and the lay orders in worship within what Lydgate calls "Cristes hool Covent."[56] Noting the frequent theme of the "mixed life" in the spiritual discourse of the period, Bartlett cites as examples Hilton's epistle to Horsley, the chapter on "The Active and the Contemplative Life" in Richard Rolle's

---

[53] Anne Clark Bartlett, "Preface," in *Yorkshire Writers: Richard Rolle of Hampole and His Followers*, ed. Carl Horstmann, new edition (London: D.S. Brewer, 1999), pages unnumbered.

[54] On Audelay, see Susanna Fein, "English Devotions for a Noble House-hold: The Long Passion in Audelay's *Counsel of Conscience*," in *After Arundel: Religious Writing in Fifteenth-Century England*, ed. Vincent Gillespie and Kantik Ghosh (Turnhout, BE: Brepols, 2011), 325–42.

[55] See Jacob Riyeff, "'Tenlvmyne' the *Laetabundus*: John Lydgate as Benedictine Poet," *Journal of English and Germanic Philology* (July, 2016): 370–93; Nicholas Heale, "John Lydgate, Monk of Bury St. Edmunds, as Spiritual Director," in The Vocation of Service to God and Neighbor, ed. Joan Greatrex (Turnhout, BE: Brepols, 1998), 59–71; W. H. E. Sweet, "Lydgate's Retraction and 'His Resorte to His Religyoun,'" in *After Arundel*, 343–59.

[56] John Lydgate, "Letabundus," in *The Minor Poems of John Lydgate, Part 1: The Religious Poems*, ed. H. N. MacCracken, EETS o.s. 107 (London: Oxford University Press, 1911), line 141.

Form of Living,[57] a treatise entitled "Our Daily Work," an allegorical composition entitled "The Abbey of the Holy Ghost," "The Charter of the Abbey of the Holy Ghost," and other extant writings.[58]

Surviving in French, Latin, and Middle English versions and printed by Wynkyn de Worde in 1531, the Middle English "The Abbey of the Holy Ghost," begins with these words:

> A dere brethir and systirs, I see þat many walde be in religyone bot þay may noghte, owthir for pouerte or for drede of thaire kyne or for band of maryage, and forthi I make here a buke of þe religeon of þe herte, þat es, of þe abbaye of the holy goste, that all tho þat ne may noghte be bodyly in religyone, þat þay may be gosteley. A Ihesu mercy, whare may þis abbay beste be funded and þis religion? Now certis, nowhare so wele als in a place þat es called Conscyence.[59]

Borrowing a phrase from Vincent Gillespie, Nicole Rice characterizes the popular "Abbey of the Holy Ghost" as answering to the laity's desire for "'para-monastic forms of spirituality'" that "translate monastic models of regulation, stability, and enclosure for their anticipated lay readers,

---

[57] See Richard Rolle, "The Form of Life," Chapter 12, in *Richard Rolle: The English Writings*, trans. and ed. by Rosamund S. Allen (New York: Paulist, 1988), 181–83.

[58] Bartlett, "Preface," in *Yorkshire Writers* (no page number given); see also Denise M. Baker, "The Active and the Contemplative Lives in Rolle, the *Cloud*-Author, and Hilton," in *The Medieval Mystical Tradition: England, Ireland, and Wales*, ed. Marion Glasscoe (Cambridge: Brewer, 1999), 85–102.

[59] *Yorkshire Writers*, 1:321.

while carefully discouraging the detachment from the world that actual cloistered life (at least in its ideal form) would entail."[60] This translative practice was not one-directional, however; it circled back to the cloister. The monastery's mirror for the laity also became a mirror in which they saw themselves, subtly transforming the self-image of monks and nuns. As Rice notes, "Although the *Abbey* was explicitly adapted for male and female readers in the world, its circulation was especially strong among vowed religious, male and female," attesting to "the contemporary blurring of boundaries between the reading practices and spiritual identities of nuns and well-off, pious laywomen."[61]

Whoever wrote the so-called *Mary Play*, included among the N-Town Plays of the fifteenth century, knew a related vernacular work, "The Charter of the Abbey of the Holy Ghost" and borrowed from it.[62] As McMurray Gibson emphasizes, many of the surviving play-texts from England have monastic ties. Henry Francis, a monk of St. Warburgh's Abbey, wrote the Chester cycle.[63] Richard Hyngham, abbot of Bury St. Edmunds, owned the Macro manuscript that contains the scripts and stage directions for the plays

---

[60] Nicole R. Rice, *Lay Piety and Religious Discipline in Middle English Literature* (Cambridge: Cambridge University Press, 2008), 17.

[61] Rice, *Lay Piety and Religious Discipline*, 137.

[62] Peter Meredith, "Introduction," in *The Mary Play from the N.town Manuscript*, ed. Peter Meredith (London and New York: Longman, 1987), 1–23, at 15, 18. Meredith refers to the study of Samuel B. Hemingway in *English Nativity Plays*, ed. Samuel B. Hemingway, Yale Studies in English 38 (New York: H. Holt, 1909).

[63] McMurray Gibson, *Theater of Devotion*, 122.

Wisdom and *Mankind;* Hyngham may even have produced the plays at Bury, which McMurray Gibson describes as a "dramatic center."[64] The Digby plays first showed up in a Bury collection.[65] While Peggy Granger casts doubt on McMurray Gibson's hypothesis that John Lydgate, monk of Bury, wrote the *Mary Play* of the N-Town manuscript, she acknowledges resemblances between his devotional poetry and the play's "liturgically-based lay piety."[66]

Richly liturgical, the *Mary Play* features English speeches punctuated by Latin chant; it employs an abbot-like character named *Contemplatio* as a stage manager who comes on-stage, blesses "þis congregacion" at the beginning and end, and speaks intermittently to the audience between scenes to give continuity to the performance.[67] Wonderfully combining contemplation and action, the enacted play presents Anne and Joachim, the parents of Mary, as a holy, idealized, tenderly loving married couple, who dedicate their sinless child to service in the Temple, where she also receives instruction, learning the psalms as English children later learned them in their primers. The dramatized interactions between Joachim and Anne, representing a devout laity, and the priests of the Temple, representing

---

[64] McMurray Gibson, *Theater of Devotion*, 107–135, at 110, 123.

[65] McMurray Gibson, *Theater of Devotion*, 126.

[66] Peggy Granger, *The N-Town Play: Drama and Liturgy in Medieval East Anglia* (Cambridge: D. S. Brewer, 2009), 170–71. See Gail McMurray Gibson, "Bury St. Edmonds, Lydgate, and the N-Town Cycle," *Speculum* 56 (1981): 56–90.

[67] *The Mary Play*, 30, 83–84. On the blessing of *Contemplatio*, see McMurray Gibson, *Theater of Devotion*, 128.

the clergy of the monastery, give expression to an idealized "mixed way" represented by Mary herself as model both for the monks, who daily sing her Magnificat at Vespers and chant the Gradual Psalms in her honor, and for the laity, who pray the same prayers in their books of hours.[68]

Translated from a chapter in the pseudo-Bonaventuran *Meditaciones vitae Christi*, the Middle English "Rule of the Life of Our Lady" describes, for example, how the Virgin Mary divided the hours of her day, alternating times of prayer and work, weaving and sewing, eating the bread of angels, and virtuously caring for her neighbors.[69] In his long poem, *Life of Our Lady*, Lydgate similarly "depicts the young Mary living in the Temple pursuing [what Rice calls] proto-monastic devotions."[70] Reared as a child in the Temple, Mary was destined also (as the dramaturgy of the *Mary Play* proclaims) to be herself the Temple, the monastery, and the Eucharistic monstrance—"full of grace" (Luke 1:28) in her soul, housing the Son of God in her very body, and bringing him into the world.

---

[68] See Duffy, *Marking the Hours*, esp. 5–13; The Mary Play, 43–46, 80–82.

[69] *Yorkshire Writers*, 1:158–161.

[70] Rice, *Lay Piety and Religious Discipline*, 138.

Learning the Monastic Way as a Mixed Life

Set before an avid lay audience, these and other vernacular works not only allowed the laity to participate in the extended life of the monasteries; they also afforded a mirror to the monks and nuns, allowing them to see and to foster their own way of life anew as a *causa exemplaris* for the laity, a "mixed life" with its own active endeavors, its own ongoing struggles for virtue, and its own, often limited achievement of the contemplative heights at which they humbly aimed.

As Nicole Rice, Allan Westphall, and others have emphasized, however, the recommendation of a "mixed life" also had an unsettling effect upon traditional hierarchies, triggering debate. For Bernard of Clairvaux, the contemplative calling was clearly the highest, a graced and disciplined anticipation already on earth of the co-citizenship of humans with the angels in Heaven.[71] If the "mixed life" was superior to the contemplative/monastic, as Thomas had argued, however, and if both prelates and laypeople were called to a "mixed" Christian life, as Hilton taught, then where did the monks and nuns of the old monasteries stand? Could they too claim a "mixed life" as monastics without betraying their own personal and collective contemplative vocation?

---

[71] See Ann W. Astell, "Introduction," in *Lay Sanctity, Medieval and Modern: A Search for Models*, ed. Ann W. Astell (Notre Dame, IN: University of Notre Dame Press, 2000), 1–26, esp. 3–8.

One prominent fifteenth-century bishop answered
"yes" to that question and offered both a theory and a
program for monastic reform. Reginald Pecock (1395–
1460)—one-time Bishop of Chichester and member of the
King's Privy Council—was the first sitting bishop in English
history to have been adjudged guilty of heresy,[72] after having
managed to offend both his fellow bishops and the religious
orders through his awkward (albeit well-intended) defense
of them against their Lollard critics.[73] As an apologetic and
instructive means, Pecock wrote his many works in both
Latin and the vernacular, with the expressed intent that
they be used in monastic schools and disseminated from
them to a wider, lay audience.[74]

Little studied today, the fifth treatise of his *Reule of
Crysten Religioun* (1443), the first of his systematic writings,
concerns the active and the contemplative lives. Like St.
Thomas and Hilton, Pecock ascribes a very high value to
the active and mixed life. Taking a theological anthropology
as his starting point, Pecock associates contemplation with

---

[72] The case is complicated, and the charges of heresy do not pertain directly to his discussion of the mixed life, except perhaps to the extent that
Pecock emphasized reason over revelation. Pecock's apologetic intention
was to give a reasonable answer to the Lollards and thus to keep them
within the fold of the Church.

[73] See Jennifer Anh-Thu Tran Smith, "Reginald Pecock and Vernacular
Theology in Pre-Reformation England" (Ph.D. dissertation, UCLA, 2012);
Charles W. Brockwell, Jr., "The Historical Career of Bishop Reginald
Pecock, D.D.: The Poore Scoleris Myrrour or a Case Study in Famous Ob-
scurity," *Harvard Theological Review* 74.2 (1981): 177–207.

[74] Reginald Pecock, *The Reule of Crysten Religioun*, ed. William Cabell
Greet, EETS o.s. 171 (London: Humphrey Milford, Oxford University
Press, 1927; repr. Kraus, 1987), 423.

human rationality, arguing that every properly human and meritorious action presupposes a prior rational recognition of something to be done and a decision of the will: "outward actijf lijf may not be had wiþoute at þe leste inparfijt contemplacioun to directe and reule hym as a liȝt to him."[75] Contemplation thus ends in a two-fold action (the "inward action" of intention and the "outward action" of realized intention),[76] which in turn provokes further contemplation and further action, until finally a perfected contemplation of God, self, and neighbor bears fruit in perfected, charitable action.[77] Even the angels in Heaven, Pecock asserts, act in God's service.[78] Uniting the contemplative Mary and the active Martha (Luke 10:38–42) thus into a single figure symbolizing "'a hool lijf,'"[79] Pecock pushes against a long-established exegetical tradition that interprets Jesus's words as exalting the contemplative life over the active.[80]

For Pecock, however, the contemplative life practiced in the monasteries—while not an end in itself—is and remains crucially important both for the personal integrity of individuals and for social and ecclesial unity. He interprets the trend of monks to leave their monasteries to

[75] Pecock, *The Reule of Crysten Religioun*, 472.

[76] Pecock, *The Reule of Crysten Religioun*, 481–82.

[77] Pecock, *The Reule of Crysten Religioun*, 473.

[78] Pecock, *The Reule of Crysten Religioun*, 495.

[79] Pecock, *The Reule of Crysten Religioun*, 478.

[80] Pecock, *The Reule of Crysten Religioun*, 488–91. Pecock teaches that outward action without contemplation and well-willing intention is without merit, while contemplation joined to well-willing is meritorious, even if circumstances prevent the outward fulfillment of the intended action.

take up tasks as parsons, vicars, and bishops as a positive fruit of their contemplative training and thus not the abandonment of a higher calling but rather its fulfillment in outward action.[81] Elsewhere in the *Reule* Pecock deals more extensively with the monasteries, holding up the example of the twelfth-century Cistercians, whose self-sustaining, "pety world" (microcosm) of the monastery featured monks skilled in a variety of crafts, monks who worked with their hands and were prepared as in a school of charity for service in the larger world of the Church as bishops and abbots.[82] As Westphall notes, Pecock emphasizes the role of the monastery as a place of education where the teaching of truth and charity is an end higher than that of psalmody per se.[83] Short, ardent, fiery prayers, Pecock instructs, can be more appropriate and effective than long ones;[84] ascetical rules can be changed to fit changed circumstances, lest they impede charitable action.[85] For this, Pecock cites the authority of "seint Benet [who] in making of his reule for monkis witnessiþ and meenyþ al þe same."[86]

Pecock, *The Reule of Crysten Religioun*, 479–80.

[82] Pecock, *The Reule of Crysten Religioun*, 419–20.

[83] Allan F. Westphall, "Reconstructing the Mixed Life in Reginald Pecock's *Reule of Crysten Religioun*," in *After Arundel*, 267–84, at 281–82. On education as the primary intention of the monastic founders, see Pecock, *The Reule of Crysten Religioun*, 422–23. On prayer and worship as a means, not an end, see Pecock, *The Reule of Crysten Religioun*, 391.

[84] Pecock, *The Reule of Crysten Religioun*, 397.

[85] Pecock, *The Reule of Crysten Religioun*, 340–41.

[86] Pecock, *The Reule of Crysten Religioun*, 341.

Clearly, as we have seen, some late medieval monks held views that resonated with Pecock's.[87] At least thirty monasteries had almoner schools, and some English monks—for example, Thomas Walsingham (d. 1422) at St. Albans and Richard Kidderminster at Winchcomb (1461–1533) —were experimenting with monastic schools that combined features of the new learning with traditions of *lectio divina* (divine reading) and that prepared people, lay and religious alike, for works of public service.[88] The cooperation of monks with local guildsmen in dramatic productions and the copying and dissemination of vernacular spiritual writings also served educational purposes expressive of a "mixed life" that endeavored to pass on to others the fruits of their contemplation.

---

[87] See Benjamin Thompson, "Monasteries, Society and Reform in Late Medieval England," in *The Religious Orders*, 165–95. Thompson observes: "The general process of monasteries opening out to society in the later Middle Ages was not only an unconscious trend, but also an overt ideal in the view of some monastic thinkers, for whom such utility was to provide further justification of the monasteries' existence" (183).

[88] See James G. Clark, *A Monastic Renaissance at St. Albans: Thomas Walsingham and His Circle c. 1350–1440* (Oxford: Oxford University Press, 2005); Clark, "Monasteries and Secular Education in Late Medieval England," in *Monasteries and Society*, 145–67; Clark, "The Religious Orders in Pre-Reformation England," 24–25; Roger Bowers, "The Almonry Schools of the English Monastery, c.1265–1540," in *Monasteries and Society in Medieval Britain: Proceedings of the 1994 Harlaxton Symposium*, ed. Benjamin Thompson (Donington, UK : Paul Watkins, 1999), 177–222; W. A. Pantin, "Abbot Kidderminster and Monastic Studies," *Downside Review* 47 (New Series 28) (1929), 198–221.

Pecock's recommendations were, however, at odds with the reforming spirit alive in the Carthusians, Bridgettines, Observant Franciscans, and hermits. Featured in my second lecture, these chose, by contrast, a reinforced, contemplative withdrawal from the world, combined with devotional and catechetical publication.

Archbishop Cranmer and the Legacy Of The Monastic Office

Rev. Dr. Bryan D. Spinks

Introduction

AT FIRST GLANCE, this title does not seem at all promising for anything beyond a five-minute statement. The Anglican Church's Offices first appeared in the 1549 *Book of Common Prayer*. Prior to 1549, from 1542, the Use of Sarum had been mandated for use in the Southern Province, and the popularity of Sarum meant in any case that the other distinctive Uses, Hereford and York, were confined to those cities and their immediate localities. These Uses were versions of the "Secular" Office, and since the monasteries had been suppressed between 1536 and 1541, the "Monastic" Use was no longer a live option. Cranmer's early life seems to have been entwined with Benedictine communities, so he was probably acquainted with the Monastic Use. However, Cranmer's views on monastic life are difficult to fathom, since practically no statements about them have survived.

His own progression in ministry in the Henrician Church identified him with the Secular clergy, and so it is doubtful that he had much interest in the monastic office when he was compiling the Offices of 1549.

Yet the history of the Divine Office as it is known at present, and particularly that of the Roman West, is more complex, and the Secular office known to Cranmer was in fact a highly monasticized Office. In order to outline the development, I will begin with some very broad brushstrokes about the Daily Office and the background to the Secular and Monastic Offices in the Roman West and regarding the Uses in England before looking in more detail at Cranmer's work on what would become the Anglican offices in the *Book of Common Prayer.*

Broad Brushstrokes

Scholarly Distinction between "Cathedral" and "Monastic" Offices

Contemporary studies of the history and development of the Daily Office, East and West, make a basic distinction between two types of office in the formative centuries.[1] The "Cathedral" Office, used by ordained clergy and staff of cathedrals, basilicas, and churches had at its core

---

[1] For overall histories, Robert Taft, *The Liturgy of the Hours in East and West. The Origins of the Divine Office and Its Meaning for Today* (Collegeville, MN: Liturgical Press, 1986); Gregory Woolfenden, *Daily Liturgical Prayer: Origins and Theology* (Ashgate, UK: Aldershot, 2004).

the recitation of set psalmody for the time of the day, canticles, praise, and intercession; the "Monastic" Office, in contrast, had at its core the continual recitation of the Psalter and the recitation of Scripture. Osmosis took place over the course of liturgical development, but as bishops came to be appointed from a monastic background, and as the monastic life became promoted as the ideal, it was the Cathedral office that became more monasticized. No pure Cathedral office or pure Monastic office has survived from late antiquity, but today the Coptic Office represents a highly monastic form, whereas the East Syrian/Church of the East form only includes Scripture readings in the office during Holy Week—preserving one hallmark of the older Cathedral Office. Furthermore, the number of hours also differs between traditions, and in some traditions, the Office is only recited in parish churches on Sunday, marking a distinction between the pastoral demands of secular clergy and the life-calling of the religious orders.

The Office in the West

The West once had different rites for the Office: Gallican, Visigothic or Hispanic, Celtic, and Roman. Of the Celtic, work has been done on this by Patricia Rumsey, but it is still shrouded in mystery.[2] For a variety

---

[2] Patricia M. Rumsey, *Sacred Time in Early Christian Ireland* (London: T&T Clark, 2007).

of reasons, the Roman rite came to displace the other rites in most places.[3] However, little is known of the early Roman Office. The re-evaluation of this document in the last forty years of the so-called Apostolic Tradition once attributed to Hippolytus means that it can no longer be invoked as Roman use of ca. 210. In current scholarship, it is with the Rule of St. Benedict that reliable information of the Roman office emerged. Benedict adopted the use of Rome, with modifications, especially with the division of the Psalter and Vigils or Matins. According to E. C. Ratcliff, it was also Benedict who introduced Prime and Compline to the former six offices of Rome.[4] However, as Jesse Billett has noted, there is nothing to indicate that any monastery in Rome was strictly "Benedictine" before the tenth century, and there is no evidence that any one rule was imposed upon monasteries.[5] The intermingling of the old Cathedral usage with Monastic usage can be traced at least to St. Gregory the Great, himself a monk, who, in order to ensure that the Office was fully observed, arranged for a monastery to be attached to St. Peter's, where the monks had the responsibility for singing daily recitation of the Office. Priests and deacons might attend and assist at certain hours, especially Lauds and Vespers, but they were

---

[3] Margot E. Fassler and Rebecca A. Baltzer (eds.), *The Divine Office in the Latin Middle Ages* (Oxford: Oxford University Press, 2000).

[4] Edward Ratcliff, "The Choir Offices," in *Liturgy and Worship*, eds. W. K. Lowther Clarke and Charles Harris (London: SPCK, 1932), 257-295.

[5] Jesse D.Billett, *The Divine Office in Anglo-Saxon England 597-1000*, Henry Bradshaw Society Subsidia (London: Henry Bradshaw Society, 2014) 5-6.

chiefly responsible for saying Mass and for attending to the pastoral offices and duties. Also, many were married and had families, which, when combined with pastoral work, made it practically impossible to maintain all the hours of prayer. This practice was also followed at the other Roman basilicas, and by the eighth century St. Peter's was served by four monasteries. The *Liber Pontificalis* records the founding of the monastery of St. Stephen Minor by Pope Stephen II (752-7) as follows:

> Meanwhile the blessed pope, ever reflecting on the things of God, had the nighttime offices, which had become slack for a long time, carried out in the hours of night, and in the same way he restored the daytime office as it had been of old. To the three monasteries which since ancient times perform this office at St. Peter's he added a fourth, and there he established monks who might thenceforth join together in the office, and he ordered an abbot over them. There he bestowed many gifts, both everything necessary for the monks in the monastery, and estates outside he established even to this day that with the other three monasteries they should chant in St. Peter's, the prince of the apostles.[6]

The Office at St. Peter's has been given fuller exposition by Peter Jeffery in his essay in the collection entitled *Old Saint Peter's, Rome*. Jeffery notes:

> ...the medieval Western Church knew two different but related ways of structuring the Divine Office, based principally on how the 150 psalms were attributed across the hours and days of the week: (1) the 'monastic *cursus*' outlined in the sixth-century Benedictine Rule but probably

---

[6] Louis Marie Oliver Duchesne, ed., *Le Libre Pontificalis: Texte, Introduction et Connentaire*, 2 vols. (Paris: E. Thorin, 1886-1892), 1, 451.

not strictly followed before the ninth century, and (2) the "Roman *cursus*," first spelled out by the ninth-century liturgical commentator Amalarius of Metz, and generally used by all non-Benedictine clergy. Both were descended from the usages of the great Roman basilicas, but by processes that can no longer be fully traced.[7]

The "Secular Use," Benedictine renewal, and the Breviary

It was in the Frankish Kingdoms under Pippin III and Charlemagne that the monastic office as used in the Roman basilicas was adopted and promoted as the rite for Royal Foundations and those churches and cathedrals served by secular canons. The canons were not monks, though they lived in community with a growing expectation that they would follow some of the practices of the religious communities, such as celibacy. This secular Office was encouraged to be adopted by Frankish monasteries too. The usage gradually spread and would also be adopted in England. What is important to understand is that this "Secular Office" was not the old "Cathedral" Office. It was itself a Monastic Office, adapted for use by cathedral and collegiate communities of canons. In the time of Bede, John the Archcantor came to Britain to train the communities at

---

[7] Peter Jeffery, "The Early Liturgy of St. Peter's and the Roman Liturgical Year," in *Old Saint Peter's Rome*, eds. Rosamund McKitterick, John Osborne, Carol M. Richardson, and Joanna Story (Cambridge: Cambridge University Press, 2013), 157-176.

Jarrow and Wearmouth to chant the Office in the Roman manner. This brings another dimension to the Office. Whatever the basic components in terms of Psalms and canticles, the type of chant and the manner of chanting also played into what was regarded as Use. The *Regular Concordia* (c.970) was compiled by Aethelwold, aided by monks from Fleury and Ghent, and was drawn up with the idea that it would serve as a common rule of life to be observed by all monasteries in England. It promoted the use of the Benedictine cursus of psalmody. It is in this period that in some minsters and cathedrals the secular clerks were expelled on the grounds of immorality, which meant they were married, and were replaced by monastic communities. This process was repeated in the Anglo-Norman church, when, for example, the secular clerks at Durham were expelled from the Anglo-Saxon cathedral in 1083, and a new cathedral was built by the Benedictines who replaced them.[8] The Benedictine story was that the secular clerks were expelled because of immorality; the historical truth is that they were bought out, and the secular priests were renumerated by the prebendary churches of the diocese.

A further development is also important: in order to avoid using many different large books for the various parts of the Office, the material was collected into one book, the Breviary. Administrators at the papal curia needed a shorter,

---

[8] For the Office when the body of Cuthbert was at Chester-le-Street, see Karen Louise Jolly, *The Community of St. Cuthbert in the Late Tenth Century: The Chester-le-Street Additions to Durham Cathedral Library* A.IV.19 (Columbus: Ohio State University Press, 2012).

more succinct office, and this gave rise to a new office, called *modernum officium*. It abbreviated and simplified the office by shortening lessons and suppressing certain responds and antiphons, though it also added new festivals to the Calendar. This abbreviated form commended itself to the Franciscans, whose itinerant calling made it difficult to join in the Office in choir with the need for a variety of large books and at particular times of the day. With approval of Pope Gregory IX, Haymo of Faversham and some other Franciscan colleagues undertook a revision with further abbreviation and material that could be carried in a single book to allow the Office to be said privately. The friars took the Roman Office and Breviary throughout Europe.[9]

England in 1548

So, what was the state of the Office in England on the eve of the Reformation? It had been known the Benedictine Office and its monastic variants until 1540/1. With the dissolution of the religious houses, the monastic form of the Roman Office came to an end. Some of the monastic churches became cathedrals, but, now with secular canons, we may presume that they used the Secular office. We know that there were differences between the Uses of Sarum, York, and Hereford. In his Preface in the Book of Common Prayer, Cranmer also mentions the Uses of Bangor and

---

[9] See Ratcliff, art.cit.

Lincoln, which was accepted at face value by nineteenth-century scholars. The recent extensive research of Nigel Morgan and Richard Pfaff has uncovered no evidence of those Uses, and there is more evidence for the Easter Bunny than there is for these two alleged Uses.[10] They perhaps had a particular procession but otherwise would have been simply versions of Sarum, perhaps like the Penpont Antiphonal of the diocese of St. David's, Wales. It is Sarum with local variants, such as the Office of St. David.[11] The use of Hereford was also in process of becoming more and more conformed to the Use of Sarum, and, as noted, from 1542 on, the southern province was mandated to use only Sarum. In the northern province of York, the Use of York seems not to have been widespread outside York minster and the city's churches. Matthew Cheung Salisbury has outlined some of the differences, such as different lessons and differences in sung texts.[12]

[10] Nigel Morgan, "The Introduction of the Sarum Calendar into the Dioceses of England in the Thirteenth century," in *Thirteenth Century England VIII: Proceedings of the Durham Conference 1999*, ed. Michael Prestwich, Richard Britnell, and Robin Frame, (Woodbridge, UK: The Boydell Press, 2001), 179-206, esp.182-3; Richard Pfaff, *The Liturgy in Medieval England. A History* (Cambridge: Cambridge University Press, 2009), pp.458, 502-5.

[11] John Caldwell, "Insular Uses Other than that of Salisbury," in (eds) Ann Buckley and Lisa Colton, *Music and Liturgy in Medieval Britain and Ireland* (Cambridge: Cambridge University Press, 2022), pp.50-82, p.80.

[12] Matthew Cheung Salisbury, *The Secular Liturgical Office in Late Medieval England* (Turnhout: BE: Brepols, 2015). See also his *The Use of York: Characteristics of the Medieval Liturgical Office in York* (York, UK: Borthwick Institute, 2008). For Hereford, William Smith, *The Use of Hereford: The Sources of a Medieval English Diocesan Rite* (London: Routledge, 2015).

What is important from these broad brushstrokes is as follows: The Office in England in 1548, whether Sarum or York, was in essence the Roman "Secular" Office, which, in spite of its name, was a monastic Office. Any revisions which used or were based on this Office was, therefore, a revision of a monastic Office.

Cranmer's Reforms of the Divine Office

Cranmer was born in July 1489 in Aslockton, Nottinghamshire, and there is a good chance that he was baptized according to the Use of Sarum. In 1503 he was sent to Cambridge to study, and the fact that he married strongly indicates that ordained ministry was not his goal. However, Cranmer stayed at Cambridge, and he was appointed "common reader" in Buckingham College (now Magdalene College) which was a Benedictine House in Cambridge. His wife died in childbirth, and he then proceeded to ordination. Susan Warbuda's biography of Cranmer reveals that he was ordained subdeacon at York in March 1515 and deacon at York Minster on April 7, 1515. In June of the same year, he was ordained priest at the conventual church of the Dominican friars in York.[13] His title or guarantee of support came from the Benedictine monastery of St. John in Colchester, Essex. He would also become a fellow of Jesus College, Cambridge. This background suggests that he might well have been aware that York had a Use different

---

[13] Susan Wabuda, *Thomas Cranmer* (London: Routledge, 2017), 25.

CRANMER AND THE MONASTIC OFFICE 49

from Sarum, and that the Dominicans and Benedictines also had a different Use, even if he was not totally aware of the exact intricate minor differences.

Cranmer was a renaissance humanist and over the course of years of study became convinced of many of the tenets embraced by the protestant causes of the continent. But he was a humanist, and he was employed by Wolsey as one of the cardinal's diplomats. This took him to Spain in 1527 and later to Italy in a bid to secure an annulment for Henry VIII's marriage to Katherine. It may be during this period that he became acquainted with the attempts to reform the Breviary. Renaissance learning had led to criticism of the barbaric Latin of the old hymns of the Breviary, and, under popes Leo X and then Clement VII, revisions were begun but never finished.[14] In 1529 Clement asked Cardinal Francis Quignon to undertake an abbreviation and revision of the Breviary to be used alongside the older Roman Breviary. Quignon was a Franciscan friar and was elected General of the Observants, and he made it his mission to end laxity amongst the friars. He was made Cardinal of the Holy Cross in Jerusalem. Quignon enlisted the help of three others: Diege Neyla, Gaspar de Castro and Genesius de Sepulveda. Clement died in 1534, and the Breviary appeared under the patronage of Pope Paul III. Quignon prepared two recensions of his reformed Breviary. The first was in 1535, which underwent eleven editions. In the light of certain

---

[14] See Bryan D. Spinks, "Renaissance Liturgical Reforms: Reflections on Intentions and Methods," in *Reformation and Renaissance Review*, Vol 7 (2005): 268-282.

objections from the Sorbonne theologians, a revised edition appeared in 1536, and underwent one hundred editions. It was used by St. Francis Xavier and was adapted by St. Ignatius Loyola for use of the Jesuits. Clearly it was popular, but it was not liked by Pope Paul IV, who forbad its use in 1558 and then outlawed it altogether in 1568. Quignon's reform was based on the belief that the center of the Office was the reading of Scripture. The Psalms were given a new distribution, with three psalms at each Office. Cranmer knew of Quignon's Breviary, and he reproduced some of the Quignon Preface in his own Preface in the Book of Common Prayer. Quignon was fiercely opposed to Henry's desire for an annulment, and it may be that Cranmer knew him from the king's business, but this opposition did not prevent Cranmer from using the cardinal's liturgical work.

In 1532 Cranmer was sent as English Ambassador to the Imperial Court of Emperor Charles in Nuremberg. It was there that Cranmer experienced the Lutheran reforms of Nuremberg, and made friends with Andreas Osiander, and married the Lutheran Reformer's niece. He experienced Osiander's reforms of the Mass and the Office, which were more conservative that Luther's own reforms. It is interesting to note that Osiander was a former Augustinian. In drawing on Quignon and Osiander, Cranmer was using the work of friars. We might loosely call his inspiration a "Franciscan-inspired" reform of the "Benedictine" Secular Office.

Cranmer's experiments

The first reforms of a liturgical nature in England are to be found in editions of Primers, or Books of Hours, intended for educated lay use. These looked much like their Catholic predecessors, but we find the inclusion of protestant material. George Joye's *Hortulus Animae* of 1529 included the Hours in English, Penitential Psalms, and commemorations, but also translations from Bucer and Luther's catechisms. While officially condemned, these primers were quite popular. However, between 1532 and 1536, Henry's marriage problems led to a break with Rome, and with this a thaw in the official attitude to such Primers. Marshall's Primer of 1534 is almost a reprint of Joye's, but includes much more material derived from Luther; a second edition includes Luther's Litany of 1529, though interpolated with invocations to saints. Hilsey's Primer was published in 1539. Thus, there were signs of liturgical reform, but in terms of the text, it was found in individual lay devotion, not in public worship.

Some years before Thomas Cranmer had the chance to implement full liturgical reforms, he had experimented with reforming the Office. Manuscript Royal 7B IV in the British Library contains two attempts by Cranmer at reform of Morning and Evening Prayer. Both are in Latin, and the second is more conservative than the first. Scheme A is probably to be dated c.1538 when Henry, for political reasons was flirting with Lutheranism. As Cuming notes, this scheme has a decidedly Lutheran flavor, though the preface shows that Cranmer has drawn on Cardinal Quignon's reforms. Geoffrey Cuming wrote:

> There are three psalms at each service, the longer ones being divided, and the three lessons go straight through the Bible chapter by chapter, starting with Genesis, Isaiah, and Matthew at Matins, and Genesis and Romans at Evensong. A fourth lesson may be added on suitable occasions. All are to be read from the pulpit, not in the chancel. The hymns are copied from the scholarly edition by Clichtoveus, of which Cranmer possessed the 1516 edition; and collects are appointed for whole seasons (as in the Nuremberg Order), not for single weeks. The Lord's Prayer and the lessons are in English, the rest in Latin. In order to make room for preaching, *Te Deum* and *Quicunque vult* may be omitted. Cranmer was already well on the way to the Daily Office of 1549.[15]

Scheme B, though more conservative, seems to date from c.1543, after Henry's so-called Catholic Reaction. In this scheme, all the Hours are kept. The manuscript is important in that it shows us a scholarly Archbishop, aware of protestant and Catholic reform movements and showing a keen sense for careful liturgical reform. Nothing came of these schemes, of course, but they illustrate Cranmer's use of Quignon and Osiander.

---

[15] Geoffrey Cuming, *A History of Anglican Liturgy* (London: Macmillan St. Martin's Press, 1969), 52.

Changes in cathedral Services

James Clark's recent study of the dissolution of the monasteries has illustrated that it was a developing work in progress, and it did not have a particularly well-planned goal when it began in 1536.[16] One outcome of the dissolution was the foundation of new cathedrals, which had their own statutes modelled more on collegiate foundations than the older cathedrals. During Edward's reign, injunctions were issued to bring the old-foundation cathedrals in line with the new foundations. Cathedrals were to keep their canons, vicars, choral or minor canons, clerks, and choristers. The injunctions altered the pattern of services. Nicholas Orme explains the changes thus:

> Matins was moved from midnight to six o'clock in the morning, the permission of 1544 now being made compulsory everywhere. The offices of prime, terce, sext and none which happened later in the morning were to be discontinued if they got in the way of sermons.[17]

The lesser hours were thus negotiable, and sermons took precedence.

---

[16] James G. Clark, *The Dissolution of the Monasteries. A New History* (New Haven and London: Yale University Press, 2022).

[17] Nicholas Orme, *The History of England's Cathedrals* (Exeter, UK: Impress, 2017), 109.

The Offices in the 1549 and 1552
Books of Common Prayer

The 1549 *Book of Common Prayer* was to come into use throughout the Church of England on Whit Sunday, June 9, 1549. It was accompanied by an Act of Uniformity, and it replaced all the previous Latin services of the Church, other than for ordination. The book began with a Preface which mainly dealt with the Divine Office and was, in places, heavily dependent upon Quignon, which Cranmer had used in his Scheme A experimental reform. Cranmer explained that the aim of the Prayer Book was to be the provision of a regular reading of Holy Scripture in order, without interruption or needless elaboration. The concern with Scripture was also shared by Quignon, as well as protestants, deriving from the humanist concern with original sources and *ad fontes* texts. Quignon had packed his revised Office with Scripture readings, and he had redistributed the Psalms to provide three at each Office. Cranmer, however, reduced the Offices to two, as he had in Scheme A of his earlier experiments, and the psalter was distributed over a month rather than a week. The Prayer Book set out a Table of Psalms to be said at Mattins and Evensong, and a Table of Lessons. A whole chapter from each Testament was read. The two services were formed by amalgamation of the older Hours. Prayer Book Matins was formed out of the old Matins or Vigil, Lauds, and Prime;

Evensong was a fusion of Vespers and Compline. There were no antiphons and responds. Much praise has been showered on Cranmer for his prose, but some of the praise is misplaced. He took many translations from the English Primers. Geoffrey Cuming cited George Joye's translation of the Lord's Prayer and of the *Te Deum* and commented: "Here at any rate the admiration usually lavished on Cranmer belons to Joye; Cranmer's only contribution was to refrain from altering Joye's phrases."[18]

Let us look in a little more detail at the two Offices. They each began with the recitation by the priest of the Lord's Prayer. Matins then began with "O Lord Open thou my lips," whereas Evensong began with "O God make speed to save me." At Matins, the *Venite,* Psalm 95, was retained from the old service as an introduction to the Psalms for the day and was used only at Matins. The 1549 rubric stated that it was to be used "without any invitatores"—that is, the seasonal refrains that were sung before Venite in the old Office. As noted, in line with Quignon and the protestant reformers, the center of the office was the recitation of Psalms and reading of Scripture, both believed to be the heart of the Office in antiquity. As noted earlier, this was erroneous. These were hallmarks of the Monastic Office, not the Cathedral Office, and thus Cranmer bequeathed the Anglican tradition a Monastic Office. In terms of exposing the faithful to Scripture, it sounds wonderful. But the modern mind is not trained to pay attention to long

---

[18] Geoffrey Cuming, *The Godly Order* (London: SPCK, 1983), 28.

readings, and one may speculate that even many sixteenth-century worshippers found it difficult as well. The readings from the two Testaments were linked by a canticle—the *Te Deum* at Matins and the *Magnificat* at Evensong. After the second reading, a second canticle was sung—the *Benedictus* at Matins and *Nunc Dimittis* at Evensong. The *Benedicite* was provided as a replacement for the *Te Deum* in Lent. In 1549 the prayers that followed began with *kyrie eleison*, the Apostles Creed, and the Lord's Prayer, followed by six pairs of versicles and responses. The salutation "The Lord be with you" and its response followed and then the collect of the day and two fixed collects. At the end of the service for Evensong, the *Quicuncque vult*, or so-called creed of St. Athanasius, was provided to be said after the *Benedictus* on certain festivals.

In 1552 certain changes were made. Matins—now called Morning Prayer—began with a Scripture sentence, an exhortation to confession, a confession, and a general absolution or declaration of God's pardon.[19] It is suggested that Evening Prayer should begin the same way, though the texts were not reprinted for that service. The *Benedicite* becomes an alternative to the *Te Deum*, and *Juilate Deo* becomes an alternative to the *Benedictus*. The Creed is recited after the second canticle: then comes the salutation and exhortation to prayer, with the kyries, the Lord's Prayer, and the six pairs of versicles and responses, and the collects. In Evening Prayer, the service still did not have "O Lord open though our lips." Psalms 98 and 67 were provided

---

[19] Alleged to be the suggestion of Peter Martyr Vermigli, but his comments on 1549 have not survived.

as alternatives to the *Magnificat* and *Nunc Dimittis*. The frequency of the *Quicunque vult* was increased by adding some more saints' days to when it should be used. One striking omission from 1549 and 1552 is the absence of hymns. Cranmer admitted that he lacked the skill to write hymns, and those that he did attempt, such as at the ordination services, confirm his claim.

The Immediate Legacy

Later tradition often reads back into earlier tradition, and this is true with Cranmer's revision of the Offices. English love of contemporary Cathedral Choral Evensong frequently shrouds history in myth. First, Cranmer's Offices, as revisions, were in many ways brilliant. However, his belief that he had restored some earlier, pristine Office, no longer tainted by Romanism, was of course, a total fantasy. What he worked with was the Secular Office, which was itself simply a Monastic Office, and two of his inspirations were humanist friars. To recite Psalms in sequence (rather than according to the time of the day) and to fill the Office with Scripture readings were Renaissance, Humanist, and Protestant convictions but, as part of the Office, were both monastic practices. Second, no music was provided other than Merbeck's short-lived unaccompanied unison setting for the 1549 text. Thus, it was for most people a *said* service. Third, few people between 1549 and 1553 owned copies of the Prayer Book, so few would have been able to recite these services daily. It was, therefore, other than Sundays, an Office for the clergy. Fourth, the two Prayer Books were short lived. In 1553 Mary came to the throne, the Latin services returned almost overnight, and with them the Use of Sarum and the Books of Hours for the laity. Cranmer bequeathed the prose texts; the establishing of these in the Anglican liturgical psyche came only gradually after 1559.

Stability And The Soul's Journey In Late Medieval English Monasticism

Dr. Ann W. Astell

A S WE HAVE SEEN, the "mixed life" was a topic of theological reflection and debate in the late Middle Ages—a topic with practical consequences for the lives of religious and lay people in England who strove to combine action with contemplation. In this second lecture we turn to another paradoxical combination in English monasticism: stability and pilgrimage. As expressions of a sacramental understanding, the outward sign of a person's vowed stability of place (*stabilitas loci*) was meant to be the means for, and the expression of, an ever-growing spiritual stability in God (*stabilitas cordis*).[1] Similarly, the outward sign of a pilgrim's physical journey to a sacred place was meant to express, to form, and to transform the soul's journey unto God. Each spiritual practice entailed its own high aims but also spiritual risks and dangers. The stable monk, on the one hand, might succumb to *acedia*, spiritual sloth, depression, or comfort-seeking—carnal deformations

---

[1] On this general topic, see James McMurry, "Monastic Stability," *Cistercian Studies* 1.2 (1966): 209–24.

59

of "resting" in God. The confused pilgrim, on the other
hand, might reduce pilgrimage to restless sight-seeing, lose
his sense of spiritual direction, or (as the Lollard critics
charged) use pilgrimage as a morally culpable evasion of
serious, charitable duties left unfulfilled at home.[2]

Benedict of Nursia's sixth-century Rule envisions
the monastery as a house of hospitality on a difficult
pilgrimage route; it does not envision the monastery itself
as the destined goal of a pilgrimage.[3] By the late Middle
Ages, however, the large monasteries in England were all
associated with saints' shrines. St. Albans housed the relics
of Saints Alban and Amphibalus, England's proto-martyrs;
Bury St. Edmunds, those of St. Edmund and of the child-
martyr, St. Robert; Westminster, the relics of St. Edward
the Confessor; Durham, the remains of St. Cuthbert and
of Godric, hermit of Finchale; Glastonbury, the relics of St.
Dunstan; Canterbury, the shrine of St. Thomas Becket. The
Cistercian abbeys at Boxley and Hailes attracted pilgrims to
venerate the Holy Rood and the Holy Blood, respectively,
and the Cluniac Priory at Bromholm was similarly famous
for its Holy Rood. The Augustinian canons at Walsingham

---

[2] Chaucer's *Canterbury Tales* depicts the scandalous motives of some pilgrims (the Pardoner, the Wife of Bath, the Merchant) en route to Canterbury. For the negative views of the Lollard priest William Thorpe regarding
pilgrimage, see the transcript of his testimony in 1407 before Archbishop
Arundel, https://chaucer.fas.harvard.edu/pages/lollard-beliefs-pilgrimages.

[3] *The Rule of St. Benedict in Latin and English, with Notes*, ed. Timothy
Fry, O.S.B. (Collegeville, MN: Liturgical Press, 1981), Chapter 53, discussed
below. Hereafter I use RB to cite the Rule.

Priory maintained the Shrine of Our Lady of Walsingham.[4] In all of these places, the seemingly opposite demands of stability and pilgrimage, of monastic withdrawal and public welcome, meet. Approaching Christ Church at Canterbury, Chaucer's pilgrims hail the Shrine of Saint Thomas Becket as a symbol of "Jerusalem celestial."[5]

Late medieval English monasteries increasingly became places of pilgrimage—the resting places of saints' bodies, of deceased patrons, and of assassinated kings like Edward II (d. 1327, buried at St. Peter's Abbey)[6] and Henry VI (d. 1471, buried at Chertsey Abbey).[7] The obligations of *stabilitas loci* were enhanced by communal, public obligations of physical and spiritual maintenance. These in turn placed pressures of various sorts—economic, ascetical, social—upon the inward stability of those maintaining the popular shrines. To what degree could stable monks or

---

[4] See Diana Webb, *Pilgrimage in Medieval England* (London: Hambledon, 2000); Islwyn Geoffrey Thomas, "The Cult of Saints' Relics in Medieval England" (Ph.D. thesis, University of London, 1977).

[5] Geoffrey Chaucer, *The Canterbury Tales*, in *The Riverside Chaucer*, ed. Larry D. Benson, 3rd ed. (Boston: Houghton Mifflin, 1987), X.51.

[6] On the efforts of Richard II to promote the cause of Edward II's canonization, see Ann W. Astell, "The Monk's Tale of Saint Edward," *Studies in the Age of Chaucer* (December, 2000): 399–405.

[7] According to Ruth Nisse, Henry VI "was being venerated as a royal martyr, with pilgrims flocking to his tomb at Chertsey Abbey." See Ruth Nisse, "'Was it not Routhe to Se?': Lydgate and the Styles of Martyrdom," in *John Lydgate: Poetry, Cult, and Lancastrian England*, ed. Larry Scanlon and James Simpson (Notre Dame, IN: University of Notre Dame Press, 2006), 279–98, at 294. See also John W. McKenna, "Piety and Propaganda: The Cult of Henry VI," in *Chaucer and Middle English Studies: in Honor of Rossell Hope Robbins*, ed. Beryl Rowland (Kent, OH: Kent State University Press, 1974), 72–88.

nuns welcome pilgrims, affording them hospitality, without themselves becoming like the guests they welcomed and like the travelling mendicants? Could persons vowed to stability themselves go on pilgrimage without violating principles of stability and enclosure? To what extent and under what conditions might a person dispense with the outward signs either of stability or of pilgrimage, without losing the complementary graces they promised to convey? Was stability opposed to pilgrimage, or was stability itself a pilgrimage, and pilgrimage ultimately stabilizing?

In what follows I heed the watchword of historian Joan Greatrex, who insists: "we need to read more intently what [religious men and women in late medieval England] read and wrote,"[8] if we hope to understand them. Drawing upon their fifteenth-century writings—the poems of John Lydgate; the translations of John Walton and of Nicholas Love; the contents of the (anonymously compiled) Carthusian miscellany and of Thomas Betson's *A Ryght Profytable Treatyse*, among others—I observe this general pattern. The Benedictine and Augustinian monks, whose outward observances of *stabilitas loci* were under duress, turned to the example of saints and martyrs who remained constant throughout various outward dislocations and trials, exemplifying stability in spirit amidst an unstable world. Contrastingly, those Bridgettine and Carthusian

---

[8] Joan Greatrex, "After Knowles: Recent Perspectives in Monastic History," in *The Religious Orders in Pre-Reformation England, Religious Orders in Pre-Reformation England,* ed. James G. Clark (Woodbridge, Suffolk, UK: The Boydell Press, 2002), 35–47, at 46.

monks who observed strict enclosure and outward stability were more drawn in their minds and hearts to themes of spiritual pilgrimage, growth, change, movement, and transformation. Each tendency can and did find validation, albeit in different ways, in the long monastic tradition.

I proceed in three parts: first, recalling what the Rule of Benedict prescribes regarding stability and pilgrimage; second, looking at the writings of two monks, John Lydgate and John Walton, who meditated upon monastic stability and defended it; third, surveying the theme of spiritual pilgrimage in the writings of Carthusian and Bridgettine monks.

Guided by the Rule of Benedict

References both to stability and to pilgrimage can be found in the Rule of Benedict. Chapter 58 instructs that candidates for admission must first be tested as to the firmness (*stabilitas*) of their resolve to live according to the Rule and then solemnly received after they promise "stability, fidelity to monastic life, and obedience."[9] Chapter 60 directs that clerics willing to take a "middle place" in the ranks of the monks may join the community, "but only if they, too, promise to keep the rule and observe stability."[10] Timothy Fry observes: "Stability adds to obedience the

---

[9] RB 58:17, 269.

[10] RB 60:8, 275.

element of perseverance in it, as well as connoting the cenobitic context and specific place in which that obedience is normally to be rendered."[11] Although the Rule itself does not distinguish, as later commentators do, between *stabilitas loci* and *stabilitas cordis*, the Rule clearly means both types in combination: "It is not simply a question of remaining physically in the coenobium throughout life, but of persevering in living the monastic life there."[12] Chapter 4 lists the various tools (*instrumenta*) for good works, beginning with the biblical commandments and including many practical imperatives fitting to monastic life, for example, "Listen readily to holy reading and devote yourself often to prayer."[13] The chapter's conclusion returns to the theme of tools and tool-use, envisioning the monastery itself as a workshop: "The workshop where we are to toil faithfully at all these tasks is the enclosure of the monastery and stability in community."[14]

The Rule clearly emphasizes the stability in community of the enclosed monk, but it also mentions the monk on pilgrimage, the *monachus peregrinus*, in three different contexts: first, the monk en route from or to his own, distant monastery, presumably on an authorized business trip, who stops at another monastery and receives its hospitality for a time (RB 61:1); second, the monk visiting from another

[11] Timothy Fry, "Appendix 5: Monastic Formation and Profession," in *The Rule of St. Benedict*, 437–77, at 465.

[12] Fry, *Rule of St. Benedict*, 464.

[13] RB 4:55–56, 185.

[14] RB 4:78, 187.

monastery who, at the end of his stay, seeks permanent admission to the new monastery (RB 61:8); third, the detestable gyrovagues, drifters who, lacking all stability in place, character, and community, wander from monastery to monastery, staying at each place for a few days before moving on (RB 1:10–11). While the gyrovague is never to be admitted, the Rule does not prohibit the acceptance of a monk from one monastery into another, provided he has the permission of his abbot; his pilgrimage is possible, apparently without loss of *stabilitas cordis*, and may be of spiritual benefit both to the monk and to the community. (It is worth remembering that Benedict himself, resigning as its abbot, left one unruly monastery in order to found his own.)[15]

The Rule also directs that honor be paid, and hospitality be given, to travelers: "Great care and concern are to be shown in receiving poor people and pilgrims, because in them more particularly Christ is received."[16] Pilgrims are to be shown "proper honor" and greeted with courtesy and prayer by the community with a kiss of peace, a bow or even "a complete prostration of the body," to signal the understanding that "Christ is to be adored [and] . . . welcomed in them."[17] As Fry notes, the heightened ceremonial observances indicate that the word "pilgrims" (*peregrines*) used in Chapter 53 of the Rule does not refer

---

[15] See Gregory the Great, *The Life of Saint Benedict / Commentary by Adalbert de Vogüé*, trans. Hilary Costello and Eoin de Bhaldraithe (Petersham, MA: St. Bede's Publications, 1993), III.2–5, 30.

[16] RB 53:15, 259.

[17] RB 53:2–7, 257.

simply to travelers, but to persons who have undertaken the difficult journey to the tombs of martyrs and saints.[18] They are to eat at the abbot's table (RB 56:1) and be provided with bedding and needed services.

The Rule is careful to instruct, however, that the care for guests must not disturb the brothers so that their other duties are neglected. The guests' quarters are to be in a separate place. A designated hostillar—a mature, God-fearing monk—is entrusted with the care of visitors. The customary silences are to be observed by the other monks: "No one is to speak or associate with guests unless he is bidden."[19]

Julie Kerr, who has studied the hospitality practiced in Cistercian houses in England, Wales, and Scotland, chronicles the high demands, financial and spiritual, placed upon the monks by the volume of pilgrims, guests, poor travelers, and sometimes even whole companies of soldiers. "The sheer number of guests that the monks provided for and the fact that communities such as Margam were overwhelmed by a continuous flow of strangers for the very reason that they were in remote places and the only source of hospitality," she writes, "suggests that the Cistercians' [social] contribution was significant and in some cases indispensable."[20] "Inherent to the Christian and monastic

[18] Fry, *Rule of St. Benedict*, p. 257, note to RB 53.2.

[19] RB 53:23, 259.

[20] Julie Kerr, "Cistercian Hospitality in the Later Middle Ages," *in Monasteries and Society in the British Isles in the Later Middle Ages*, ed. Janet Burton and Karen Stöber (Woodbridge, Suffolk, UK: The Boydell Press, 2008), 25–39, at 38.

life," hospitality nonetheless clearly "needed to be controlled lest the presence of outsiders and their entertainment within the precinct led the monks astray."[21] Negotiating this balance was certainly not easy.

Two Pilgrim Monks in Praise of Stability: Lydgate and Walton

The large Benedictine abbey at Bury St. Edmunds offered its lavish hospitality to the twelve-year-old boy-king Henry VI at Christmas, 1433—a royal visit and extended pilgrimage that lasted until Easter, 1434. Among the entertainments offered the king were John Lydgate's English versifications in rhyme royal of five royal charters granted to the monastery by previous kings of England: Canute, Hardecanute, Edward the Confessor, William the Conqueror, and Henry I. As Reginald Webber explains in detail, Lydgate's *Cartae Versificatae* (versified charters) were part of Abbot William Curteys's "personal campaign to reestablish royal support for the abbey,"[22] in the wake of some recent disapproving gestures by Henry V, who had urged monastic reform, and amidst the monastery's local controversies over jurisdiction with William Alnwick, then

---

[21] Kerr, "Cistercian Hospitality in the Later Middle Ages," 39.

[22] Reginald Webber, "*Judas non dormit*: John Lydgate and Late-Medieval Benedictine Episcopal Conflicts—Part II," *American Benedictine Review* 61 (2010): 81–94, qtd. at 91.

Bishop of Norwich.[23] The versified charters, together with Lydgate's poetic hagiography, *The Lives of Sts. Edmund and Fremond*—a magnificent copy of which was later presented to the king[24]—may be seen as the monks' communal defense both of the principle of *stabilitas loci* and of pilgrimage to the monastery's patron saint, practices they deemed spiritually important not only for themselves but for king and country.

Lydgate is regularly named "monk of Bury" by his contemporaries, and his attachment to that monastery perdured from his youth, despite his apparently many peregrinations. Born near the abbey, he studied at the monastery's almonry school and entered the novitiate at fifteen after having a religious experience before a crucifix in the cloister, with the word "Vide" ("Behold!") written beside it—an experience the aged Lydgate relates in an autobiographical poem, known to us as "The Testament of Dan John Lydgate." Professed in 1387 at age sixteen, Lydgate was finally ordained a priest ten years later in 1397.

While studying at Gloucester College at Oxford for the two years generally prescribed for Benedictine scholars (1406–1408), he came into contact with the Prince of Wales, the future Henry V, who commissioned him in 1412 to do a poetic translation into English of Guido della Colonna's

---

[23] The monks at Bury had not initially supported the succession of Henry IV to the throne, and they disapproved of England's war with France. Under Archbishop Arundel's *Constitutions*, Bishop Alnwick claimed the right to conduct trials against heretics in Bury—a right the abbot contested.

[24] Jennifer Sisk, "Lydgate's Problematic Commission—A Life of St. Edmund for Henry VI," *Journal of English and Germanic Philology* 109.3 (2010): 349–75.

Historia Destructionis Troiae; Lydgate's massive *Troy Book*
thus came to be. Henry V then commissioned Lydgate's *The*
Life of Our Lady, and the monk almost certainly composed
The Siege of Thebes for that same king. Other known
patrons of the poet include Richard Beauchamp, earl of
Warwick; Thomas Montacute, earl of Salisbury; Princess
Isabell, countess of Warwick; Margaret Talbot, countess of
Shrewsbury; Humphrey, duke of Gloucester (for whom he
wrote *The Fall of Princes*); Jacqueline, countess of Hainault
and Holland; and, of course, Henry VI.[25]

Lydgate's highly unusual career as a Lancastrian "poet
laureate" places him away from Bury St. Edmunds for
certain periods of time: at Oxford (1406–1408), in Paris
(1426), at Hatfield Priory in Essex (1423–1430), where
Lydgate also served as prior for a few years, and in London
(1432?). According to Derek Pearsall, "Lydgate was probably
in Bury on a permanent basis by the time of the royal visit"
of Henry VI in 1433–1434.[26] To what extent Lydgate was
actually away from Bury's cloister before that cannot be
determined from his many commissions, however. Pearsall
cautions, "We should be wary of assuming too readily that
he was a frequent visitor in society," given the strictures of
monastic discipline and the fact that "Bury itself . . . received
a constant stream of visitors."[27]

---

[25] See Derek Pearsall, *John Lydgate (1371–1449): A Bio-bibliography*, English Literary Studies 71 (Victoria, CA: University of Victoria, 1997).

[26] Pearsall, *John Lydgate*, 34.

[27] Pearsall, *John Lydgate*, 21.

Did Lydgate himself feel that his eccentric career as a court poet was at odds with his Benedictine vocation to *stabilitas loci* and *stabilitas cordis*? As Ruth Nisse and W. H. E. Sweet have argued, the "Testament" Lydgate composed in his old age humbly confesses his shortcomings as a monk and voices his sincere regret at having written at such length on secular themes—the matters of Greece, Troy, and Rome; it also points indirectly to the greater significance of the devotional works among the so-called "minor poems" that the monk of Bury wrote, many of which date from his last years, when he was certainly in residence at the monastery.[28] In the "Testament" itself, the "I" of the repentant, autobiographical poet loses itself finally in the "I" of Christ speaking from the cross, proclaiming himself merciful and encouraging the contrite soul: "Go eche day onward on thy pylgrymage."[29]

Lydgate's three-part *Lives of Sts. Albon and Amphibalus* (*SSAA*), commissioned by John Whethamsted, abbot of St. Albans, arguably enfolds Lydgate's own conversion story as monk and poet in that of the two early Christian, English martyrs whose relics were enshrined at St. Albans. As a foreshadowing of Albon's later colors as a baptized and

---

[28] W. H. E. Sweet, "Lydgate's Retraction and 'his resorte to his religyoun,'" in *After Arundel: Religious Writing in Fifteenth-Century England*, ed. Vincent Gillespie and Kantik Ghosh (Turnhout, BE: Brepols, 2011), 343–359; Nisse, "'Was it not Routhe to Se?': Lydgate and the Styles of Martyrdom," in *John Lydgate: Poetry, Cult, and Lancastrian England,* cited above.

[29] "The Testament of Dan John Lydgate," in The Minor Poems of John Lydgate, Part 1, ed. Henry Noble MacCracken, E.E.T.S. e. s. 107 (1911; repr. 2002), 329–362, at line 892.

martyred Christian, Lydgate presents the colors of Albon's clothing when he is ritually inducted as a Roman soldier — white (for pure intent and meekness) and red (for sacrificial readiness to die).[30] Anke Bernau rightly observes that Lydgate associates these colors with the rhetorical "colors" used by the poet in his aureate metaphors and similes.[31] What Bernau misses is the degree to which Lydgate would have identified the future martyr's ritual clothing as a soldier with the rite of Lydgate's own monastic profession, which, as Michael Casey instructs, was regarded from the time of Jerome as a "second baptism" and a species of martyrdom.[32] Albon's head is shaved (1:438); he is bathed (1:442–48) before his ritual clothing; he takes four military vows (1:568–581)—vows later voided and superseded by his baptismal vows. The colors "white and blak" (1:99) that

[30] John Lydgate, *Saint Albon and Saint Amphibalus*, ed. George F. Reinecke (New York: Garland, 1985), Book 1, lines 64–79, 479–483, 521–532. Hereafter, I cite this edition parenthetically by book and line number.

[31] Developing a suggestion from Jennifer Sisk about Lydgate's innovation as a hagiographer, Anke Bernau underscores the "radical newness" that the genre affords the poet. See Anke Bernau, "Lydgate's Saintly Poetics," in Sanctity as Literature in Late Medieval Britain, ed. Eva von Contzen and Anke Bernau (Manchester, UK: Manchester University Press, 2015), 151–171, at 166; Sisk, "Lydgate's Problematic Commission—A Life of St. Edmund for Henry VI," cited above. Bernau deals specifically with SSAA.

[32] Michael Casey, *An Unexciting Life: Reflections on Benedictine Spirituality* (New York: Fordham University Press, 2005), 265. See also Edward Eugene Malone, *The Monk and the Martyr: The Monk as the Successor of the Martyr* (Washington, DC: The Catholic University of America Press, 1950), esp. 112–43; Polycarpus A. Aydin, *The Syriac Order of Monastic Profession and the Order of Baptism* (Piscataway, NJ: Gorgias Press, 2017). Martin Luther explicitly rejected the idea of a second baptism—a topic that remains current in ecumenical discussions today. See Heinrich Bacht, S.J., "Die Mönchsprofess als Zweite Taufe," in *Catholica: Vierteljahrsschrift für Ökumenische Theologie* (Münster: Ashendorff, 1969): 240–77.

mark the monk's humble writing double as his monastic colors: white (for his renewed Baptismal commitment through his vows of poverty, chastity, and obedience) and black (the color of his Benedictine robe). Like the martyr who shifts his allegiance from Diocletian to Christ, Lydgate the converted monk-poet turns from classical models to a new poetry, inspired by the passions of the martyrs, that embraces a plain style "voide of al colours sauff rude colours blake" (1:929).

Reflective of his own monastic commitment to *stabilitas*, Lydgate's poem repeatedly characterizes Albon and his friend and mentor, the monk-like Amphibalus, as "stable" in virtue, because there is "no stabilnesse . . . without vertu" (2:852–55). Albon's baptism makes him "stable bi perfit charite" (2:746). "Stable in his intent" (2:916), his spiritual armor "forgid with stabilnesse" (2:976), Albon under arrest clings to his cross, which is "as any centre stable" (2:1012); his faith "so stable" (2:1725), he stands his ground like "that hous bilt on a stable ston" (2:1166). Amphibalus, too, shows "his herte stable, strong as a diamaunt" (3:960); dying at the stake, he stands erect, "stable in praier and in his orisoun" (3:1146). The faithful friendship between Albon and Amphibalus as brothers in Christ joined in their separate martyrdoms symbolizes yet another monastic value, that of the common life as a seedbed for the great communion of saints.

Lydgate closes the poem with his own prayer to St. Albon, begging his intercession for "the syxt Henry" (3:1564) and for all the people of England in their various ranks and occupations. In the version of the prayer later printed at St. Albans in 1534, another poet has substituted a petition to England's protomartyr for Henry VIII, his spouse "quene Anna," and their daughter, princess Elizabeth.[33]

In her own unstable times, Elizabeth translated Boethius's *Consolatio philosophiae* into English, following in the tradition of Chaucer and John Walton, an Augustinian canon of Oseney Abbey, Oxfordshire.[34] Historian James Clark calls Walton "the only really significant scholar of the later Middle Ages."[35] A contemporary record associated with his being granted special permission to hold a second benefice, describes him as a religious zealous in life and customs ("religionis zelus vite et morum").[36] As a beneficed papal chaplain, however, Walton was pulled to some degree out of the orbit of regular monastic life—a situation that inspired him, like Lydgate, to reflect seriously on the meaning of monastic stability.

His best-known work, a brilliant poetic translation in 1410 of Boethius's *Consolation of Philosophy*, was commissioned by Elizabeth Berkeley, countess of

---

[33] See Lydgate, *Saint Albon and Saint Amphibalus*, 208.

[34] See *Consolation of Queen Elizabeth I: The Queen's Translation of De Consolatione Philosophiae*, ed. Noel Harold Kaylor, Jr. and Philip Edward Philips (Tempe: Arizona Center for Medieval and Renaissance Studies, 2009).

[35] James G. Clark, "The Religious Orders in Pre-Reformation England," in *Religious Orders in Pre-Reformation England*, 3–33, at 21.

[36] Mark Science, "Introduction," in *Boethius: De Consolatione Philosophiae, Translated by John Walton*, ed. Mark Science, EETS o.s. 170 (London: Humphrey Milford, Oxford University Press, 1927, repr. 1998), vii–lxvii, at xlvii.

Warwick.[37] Like Lydgate in his hagiographies of martyrs, Walton presents Boethius as a Christian martyr and a model for monks whose own vocation demands of them a meditative life of study and prayer. Citing the example of Jerome, Walton refuses to imitate pagan poets by invoking their muses. Introducing his translation with a life of Boethius, Walton describes him as a martyr who dared to protest against the vices of the emperor and who, falsely accused of treason, died for the Catholic faith at the order of an Arian heretic. The translator's preface to Books IV and V of the *Consolation* paraphrases Romans 11:34: "Who wist his witt when he þis world began? / Or who was he þat was his conseillour?"[38]

Under house arrest, distraught at the sudden change in his fortunes, and facing execution, the prisoner Boethius has difficulty recalling the content of all the wise books he has read—the books on the shelves of his library and in the Augustinian "library" of his memory.[39] He has forgotten his own eternal destiny. Lady Philosophy prompts his remembrance with her questions, reminding him of his belief in God's goodness and governance. She contrasts the "stabilnesse" of Lady Fortune, equipped with her ever-

---

[37] See Heather A. Reid, "Patronness of Orthodoxy: Elizabeth Berkeley, John Walton, and the Middle English Storie of Asneth, a West Midlands Devotional Text," *Medieval Church Studies* (2014): 405–441.

[38] *Boethius: De Consolatione Philosophiae, Translated by John Walton,* ed. Mark Science, EETS o.s. 170 (London: Humphrey Milford, Oxford University Press, 1927, repr. 1998), 210, stanza 575.

[39] *Boethius: De Consolatione Philosophiae,* 50, stanza 129. See Book 10 of Augustine's *Confessions.*

turning wheel, with the stability of God, the unmoved Mover, who rests at the still center of the circle.[40] (Lady Fortune's stability is, paradoxically, her constant mutability.) By the fifth book of the dialogue, Lady Philosophy has helped the suffering prisoner to regain his own stability—the "verray stabilnesse" from which he has fallen—by turning to God who "chaungeþ noght."[41]

Boethian stability is thus not so far removed from Benedictine stability as one might at first think. In his influential commentary on the *Consolation of Philosophy,* the Benedictine scholar Remigius of Auxerre (ca. 841–908) likens Saint Benedict's nocturnal vision of the "whole world . . . in a single ray" of light,[42] on the one hand, to Lady Philosophy's description of God's providential comprehension of all things "wholly and simultaneously" [*tota simul*] from eternity, on the other.[43] The Cistercian abbot Aelred of Rievaulx echoes the *Consolation* in sermons on the feast of Benedict, likening the way of wisdom pointed out by Lady Philosophy to the way prescribed by the Rule.[44]

---

[40] *Boethius: De Consolatione Philosophiae,* 63, stanza 162; 70, stanza 180; 260, stanza 744.

[41] Ibid, 323, stanza 960.

[42] Gregory the Great, *The Life of Saint Benedict / Commentary by Adalbert de Vogüé,* Chapter XXXV.3, 164.

[43] In *Cons.* 5, pr. 6, 4, Philosophia defines eternity as "the simultaneous and complete [*tota simul et perfecta*] possession of infinite life," Boethius, *Consolation of Philosophy,* trans. W. V. Cooper (London: J. M. Dent, 1902), 115.

[44] See Ann W. Astell, "Consolations of Friendship: The Augustinian Reception of Boethius in Twelfth-Century England," in *The Legacy of Boethius in Medieval England: The Consolation and Its Afterlives,* ed. A. Joseph McMullen and Erica Weaver (Tempe: Arizona Center for Medieval and Renaissance Studies, 2018), 103–24.

Translating the *Consolation* in the fifteenth century, Walton finds a Benedictine stability in the martyr Boethius, who learns and proclaims: "To triste in god it is no þing in veyne / . . . / For he refuseth neuere a lowely bone."[45]

Amidst unstable times, some Benedictine monks, like Boethius imprisoned in his cell, became recluses within the premises of their monasteries. David Knowles points to the case of the recluse of Westminster, to whom Richard II made his confession, and to recluses at Durham, Sherborne, and Worcester.[46] These men of silence provided anchors for their monastic and parish communities, parallel to the case of Dame Julian (1343–1422?), the visionary anchoress of Norwich, who may well have been a Benedictine nun at Carrow Priory. The parish church and the priory were only a mile's distance from each other; the nuns at the priory instructed local girls; and Carrow is known to have supported anchoresses.[47] The priory is believed to have endowed the anchorhold at the parish church. (Julian's *Shewings* reappeared in the seventeenth century in Cambrai, among Benedictine nuns exiled from England.)[48]

---

[45] *Boethius: De Consolatione Philosophiae*, 325, stanzas 1000–1001.

[46] Dom David Knowles, *The Religious Orders in England, Vol. 2: The End of the Middle Ages,* 3 vols. (Cambridge: Cambridge University Press, 1955), 2:219.

[47] Nicholas Watson and Jacqueline Jenkins, "Introduction," in *The Writings of Julian of Norwich*, ed. Nicholas Watson and Jacqueline Jenkins (University Park: Pennsylvania State University Press, 2006), 4–5.

[48] For the Cambrai manuscripts, see *The Writings of Julian of Norwich,* 437–448.

Various forms of eremitical life throve in fourteenth-
and fifteenth-century England. Alongside the Benedictine
and Augustinian recluses, there were individual laypersons
who made their monastic profession before the bishop
according to the Rule of St. Paul the Hermit or of St.
Celestine.[49] Others were inspired by the example of
Richard Rolle, hermit of Hampole, to whose authorship
several eremitical rules were ascribed.[50] And there were the
Carthusians, whose Rule establishes what Jessica Brantley
calls "a community of solitaries."[51]

The Soul's Journey: Love's Mirror, One Monk's Miscellany, and Betson's Treatise

Nicholas Love, the Carthusian prior of Mount Grace
in Yorkshire, was a *monachus peregrinus* of the sort clearly
approved by the Rule of St. Benedict. A former Benedictine
monk at Crowland Abbey,[52] Love left the Benedictines for
the Carthusians, climbing up the ascetical ladder to the

---

[49] Virginia Davis, "The Rule of Saint Paul, the First Hermit, in Late Medieval England," in *Monks, Hermits, and the Ascetic Tradition: Papers Read at
the 1984 Summer Meeting and the 1985 Winter Meeting of the Ecclesiastical
History Society,* ed. W. J. Sheils (Oxford: Basil Blackwell, 1985), 203–214.

[50] See Hope Emily Allen, *Writings Ascribed to Richard Rolle, Hermit of
Hampole* (London: Oxford University Press, 1927), 324–29, 329–33.

[51] Jessica Brantley, *Reading in the Wilderness: Private Devotion and Public
Performance in Late Medieval England* (Chicago: University of Chicago
Press, 2007), 12.

[52] See Michael G. Sargent, "Nicholas Love as an Ecclesiastical Reformer,"
Church History and Religious Culture 96 (2016): 40–64, esp. 56–58.

charterhouse, which established a community of hermits.[53] In late medieval England, "parish priests, distinguished clerks, monks, and canons of every order [passed] into the Charterhouse," notes David Knowles, and these were "often men of years and of formed character."[54]

Unlike the Benedictine, Augustinian, and Cistercian houses, the charterhouses were relatively few, small, and recent foundations—the London charterhouse dates from 1371; Mount Grace was founded by Thomas Holland, Duke of Surrey, in 1398, at the end of Richard II's reign; the charterhouse at Sheen followed in 1414, under the auspices of Henry V. The charterhouses were not pilgrimage sites. Intent on solitude, silence, and withdrawal, the Carthusians practiced a strict monasticism that drew the admiration of the faithful, many of whom wanted, as confraternity members, to be buried on the grounds.[55] Located on a pilgrimage route between York and Durham, Mount Grace did, however, maintain houses of hospitality for pilgrims, setting at some risk its own difficult-to-maintain, contemplative ideals, but winning popular appreciation.[56]

Nicholas Love, Prior at Mount Grace, is chiefly famous as the author in 1410 of the influential Middle English work,

---

[53] See Brantley, *Reading in the Wilderness,* on "the hierarchy of asceticism by which the pope permitted monks of other (ostensibly lower) orders to enlist in the life of the charterhouse without breaking their original vows" (11).

[54] Knowles, *Religious Orders,* 2:138.

[55] Glyn Coppack, "'Make straight in the desert a highway for our God': The Carthusians and Community in Late Medieval England," in *Monasteries and Society,* 168–79, esp. 169–73.

[56] Coppack, "'Make straight in the desert a highway for our God,'" 176–77.

The Mirror of the Blessed Life of Jesus Christ, a translation
and adaption of the pseudo-Bonaventuran *Meditationes
Vitae Christi*. Licensed for publication by Archbishop
Thomas Arundel, the *Mirror* has in recent years generally
been characterized as an anti-Lollard writing.[57] Love does
indeed lambast the Lollards, especially on those pages
where the Carthusian author meditates on the Last Supper
and, in a concluding treatise, on the Blessed Sacrament. As
Michael Sargent, editor of the critical edition of the text, has
forcefully argued, however, the *Mirror* cannot be reduced
to this agenda. Rather, it stands as a remarkable work in the
vernacular that is consistent with Love's other, "eventually
unsuccessful attempt[s] at monastic reform in England."[58]
As Sargent has demonstrated, Love was among those who
urged Henry V, upon his return from France in 1421, to
convene the extraordinary meeting at Westminster of over
350 Black Friars (monks and prelates), calling them to
reform in thirteen articles.[59] These articles (in the words of
Knowles) present "a carefully devised and practical attack
on recognized abuses."[60] Aimed at correcting disciplinary
violations in attire, diet, and cloister, the statutes recall

---

[57] See, for example, David Aers and Lynn Staley, *The Powers of the Holy:
Religion, Politics, and Gender in Late Medieval English Culture* (University Park: Pennsylvania State University Press, 1996); Nicholas Watson,
"Censorship and Cultural Change in Late Medieval England: Vernacular
Theology, the Oxford Translation Debate, and Arundel's Constitutions of
1409," *Speculum* 70 (1995): 822–64.

[58] Sargent, "Nicholas Love as an Ecclesiastical Reformer," 40.

[59] Sargent, "Nicholas Love as an Ecclesiastical Reformer," 49–53.

[60] Knowles, *Religious Orders*, 2:184.

monasticism's own aims and ideals as a regulated following of Christ.

Love's *Mirror* directs the reader's attention more obviously to Christ, presenting him in affective terms as deserving of the heartfelt, "carnal" love that, "as seint Bernard seith,"[61] necessarily precedes and grounds the soul's "spiritual" love of him.[62] The *Mirror* aims at the stirring of devotion. In a series of guided meditations, the *Mirror* invites readers to use their imagination to picture the vividly described persons and scenes and to hear the spoken words scripted for them through the "dyuerse ymaginacious of cristes lyf" contained in the book.[63] While this authorial guidance limits the reader's imagination to some degree,[64] it works effectively to make the reader an audience member present with others at an interior mystery play—a dramatic analogy that fits well with Jessica Brantley's analysis of the so-called Carthusian miscellany.[65]

[61] Nicholas Love, *The Mirrour of the Blessed Lyf of Jesu Christ*, 2 vols. (Salzburg, AT: Institut für Anglistik und Amerikanistik, Universität Salzburg, 1989), 8. Here and throughout, I have silently changed the "long s" of the Middle English script into the "s" of contemporary typography.

[62] See Bernard of Clairvaux, *On the Song of Songs 1*, trans. Kilian Walsh (Kalamazoo, MI: Cistercian Publications, 1971), Sermon 20.v.6: "Notice that the love of the heart is, in a certain sense, carnal, because our hearts are attracted most toward the humanity of Christ and the things that he did and commanded while in the flesh."

[63] Love, *Mirrour*, 9.

[64] On this point of limitation, see Michelle Barnes, "Love and Medieval Meditations on Christ," *Speculum* 82.2 (2007): 380–408.

[65] See Brantley, *Reading in the Wilderness*, cited above.

Love's *Mirror* did, in fact, inspire the parliament scene in the N-Town *Mary Play*.[66] Rather than beginning with the Annunciation scene, the *Mirror* begins with a dramatic, extra-biblical parliament in Heaven in which the Archangel Gabriel, speaking on behalf of the angels assembled before the Father's throne, begs him to commence the long-awaited time of grace when the empty seats of the fallen angels are to be filled with redeemed human beings. The four personified daughters of the divine King—Mercy, Truth, Justice, and Peace—then voice their support for, and objections to, humanity's redemption. Finding no angel or human able to accomplish a just and merciful reconciliation, a personified Reason asks the Triune God to accomplish this work in the Person of the Son. The agreement of the three divine Persons is then followed by the kissing and embracing of the four daughters. Love explains that this "processe schal be taken as in liknesse and oneliche as a manere of a parable and deuou3t ymagynacioun stirynge man to loue god souereynly for his grete mercye to man and his endeles godenesse."[67]

What I want to emphasize here is that placing this heavenly scene first allows Love to structure the *Mirror* as a whole according to the *exitus-reditus* pattern, which begins with the divine descent of the Eternal Word-made-flesh (his *exitus* from Heaven) and ends with the bodily Ascension of the Lord, who returns to the Father, accomplishing his

---

[66] See Peter Meredith, "Introduction" in *The Mary Play from the N.town Manuscript,* ed. Peter Meredith (London and New York: Longman, 1987), 15, 18, and Meredith's endnotes, 108–16.

[67] Love, *Mirrour,* 19.

reditus (return to Heaven) and leading the way heavenwards for a redeemed humanity. Love does include a short final meditation on Pentecost and does attach to the *Mirror* an English treatise *De Sacramento Corporis Christi* (*Concerning the Sacrament of the Body of Christ*), but his long meditation on the Ascension treats it explicitly as the greatest of the feasts, the triumphal conclusion of the blessed life of Jesus Christ. Love invites his readers to understand with heartfelt emotion that the Lord is passing away from them in his bodily presence, "the tyme of his pilgrimage here on erthe . . . fully complete and ended."[68]

The *exitus-reditus* pilgrimage of Jesus Christ thus provides the basis for the readers' meditative participation in that same pilgrimage in space and time. The individual mysteries of Christ's earthly life place the reader imaginatively in the holy places in Galilee and Judea where Jesus lived, worked, taught, suffered, died, rose from the dead, and ascended into heaven. Together with Mary and the disciples, the readers encounter him anew, "kissynge deuoutly the steppes of his feete where he laste touched the erthe."[69]

Combining this pilgrimage in space with a temporal one, Love divides the chronologically arranged mysteries into meditations assigned to the different days of the week. For Monday there are nine meditations, from the parliament in heaven to the purification of Mary after Christ's birth;

[68] Love, *Mirrour*, 2:285.

[69] Love, *Mirrour*, 2:297.

for Tuesday, five meditations, from the flight into Egypt until the Lord's baptism in the Jordan; for Wednesday, ten meditations on Christ's fasting, his call of the disciples, his first miracles and public teaching; for Thursday, fifteen meditations, beginning with the multiplication of the loaves and fishes and ending with the Last Supper; for Friday, nine meditations on Christ's passion, death, and burial; for Saturday, fifteen meditations on Christ's resurrection, appearances to his disciples, Ascension, and sending of the Holy Ghost. There are no prescribed meditations for Sunday, unless the appended treatise on the Blessed Sacrament (Chapter 64) is understood as fitting for that paradoxically timeless day that, week by week, anticipates the eternal Sabbath rest in the divine presence.

Since the proper use of each meditation requires a time of silence and withdrawal from "alle othere occupaciouns and besynesse,"[70] Love emphasizes that the reader is not actually expected to use all of these meditations on the prescribed days over the course of a single week, but to draw upon them selectively, day by day, "as it semeth moste coumfortable and stirynge to his deuocioun."[71] He suggests, for example, that the meditations for Monday might be used appropriately during the season of Advent.[72] Suitable for Passiontide, the Friday meditations explicitly mark the liturgical hours, from Matins at the hour of Jesus' arrest

---

[70] Love, *Mirrour*, 1:12.

[71] Love, *Mirrour*, 2:300; 1:12.

[72] Love, *Mirrour*, 1:13.

to Compline, the hour of his burial. Occupied thus with meditation, like Saint Cecilia who (Love writes) kept the Gospel of Christ hid in her breast,[73] the devout Christian becomes better able not only to resist vain thoughts and worldly temptations, but also to practice virtue in imitation of Christ.

Writing in the vernacular, Love clearly envisions a lay audience of "simple and deuout soules,"[74] but monks and nuns also read the *Mirror* and copied it for others to read. As Karnes notes, "Both the *Mirror of the Blessed Life of Jesus Christ* . . . and its source enjoyed tremendous popularity, as indicated by the survival of the *Meditationes* in 217 manuscripts and the *Mirror* in 64," and by the *Mirror*'s being printed "at least ten times between 1484 and 1606."[75]

Love was himself the first reader of the *Mirror*, and there are clear signs that he intended it not only for the spiritual formation of the laity but also as a means for monastic reform. In the chapter that meditates on Martha and Mary, for example, Love follows a long tradition in associating Martha with the active life, Mary with the contemplative. He praises the active life and the mixed life, citing Walter Hilton and recommending Hilton's epistolary treatise on the topic.[76] But Love goes beyond this, first, to criticize

---

[73] Love, *Mirrour*, 1:10.

[74] Love, *Mirrour*, 1:13.

[75] Karnes, "Love and Medieval Meditations on Christ," 383.

[76] Love, *Mirrour*, 2:165.

men and women "in the astate of contemplatyf lyffe"[77] that scandalously fail to be true contemplatives because they have neglected the active life that strives for virtue; second, to recommend to contemplatives the indispensable virtues of humility, patience, and keeping silence.[78]

As hermits living in a communal setting, Carthusians like Nicholas Love definitely belonged to the contemplative state, but they also understood their state of life to overflow into charitable action through copying devotional and catechetical manuscripts in their cells—an activity they called "preaching with hands."[79] "This oscillation between the most private of eremitical devotions and a demonstrated engagement with more public, pastoral concerns," writes Jessica Brantley, "is a hallmark of late-medieval Carthusian piety, and it finds reflection both in the verbal and in the visual arts."[80]

Examples abound. Besides Love's *Mirror*, the *Speculum Devotorum* by a Carthusian at Sheen Priory might be cited.[81] Studied in detail by Jessica Brantley, the

---

[77] Love, *Mirrour,* 2:160.

[78] Love, *Mirrour,* 2:163–65.

[79] Felix Heinzer, "Preaching with the Hands: Notes on Cassiodorus' Praise of Handwriting and Its Medieval Reception," in *Exploring Written Artefacts: Objects, Methods, and Concepts,* ed. Jörg B. Quenzer (Berlin, Boston: DeGruyter, 2021), 947–64.

[80] Brantley, *Reading in the Wilderness,* 22.

[81] *A Mirror to Devout People: Speculum devotorum,* ed. Paul J. Patterson, E.E.T.S. o.s. (Oxford: Oxford University Press, 2016). See also Paul J. Patterson, "Female Readers and the Sources of the Mirror to Devout People," *Journal of Medieval Religious Cultures* 42.2 (2016): 181–200.

illustrated prayer book copied by another unnamed English Carthusian—British Library Addition MS 37049—includes such a wealth of material that Douglas Gray has called it a "spiritual encyclopedia."[82] Among these are many of the poems by Richard Rolle, the famous hermit of Hampole, and writings attributed to him; translations from Henry Suso's *Horologium sapientiae*; verses on Christ's numbered wounds and on his holy name; poems on Mary's name, her joys, and her miracles; dialogues between body and soul; verses on the founding of the Carthusian Order, on Active and Contemplative Life; plus a long, chiefly catechetical work entitled "The Desert of Religion," filled with trees whose branches enumerate virtues, vices, creedal articles, gifts of the Spirit, etc.

With its opening images of a Byzantine Virgin, a Byzantine Christ, a *Mappa Mundi*, and a copied excerpt from Mandeville's *Travels* about Jerusalem, however, it might better be described as a work of spiritual pilgrimage. Brantley notes that a two-sided banner of Jesus and Mary was carried at the head of the processions of novices at Syon Abbey, as a sign of their desire to follow both Christ and Mary.[83] The closing items in the manuscript also form a recognizable meditative sequence, with copied excerpts from the Middle English *Pilgrimage of a Soul* (a dream

---

[82] Douglas Gray, "London, British Library, Additional MS 37049—A Spiritual Encyclopedia," in *Text and Controversy from Wyclif to Bale: Essays in Honour of Anne Hudson*, ed. Helen Barr and Ann M. Hutchinson (Turnhout, BE: Brepols, 2005), 99–116.

[83] Brantley, *Reading in the Wilderness*, 177.

vision about one person's death, his soul's judgment, his passage through purgatory, and entrance into paradise), followed by counsels against despair, and a final treatise on God's mercy and justice.[84]

Closely associated with the charterhouse at Sheen, the Bridgettine monastery at Syon, founded by Henry V as part of his program of monastic reform, was famous for its well-stocked library, inclusive of works by Humanist writers like Erasmus, and for its attraction of exemplary members, among them respected scholars from the universities who sought out the monastery's solitude.[85] While the nuns of Syon looked to the Virgin Mary as their exemplar, the monks of that double-monastery seem to have taken the eremitical scholar-saint Jerome, pilgrim to Bethlehem, as their model and patron. Simon Wynter, one of the first of the brethren at Syon, had composed a life of Jerome (c. 1430) that records his scholarly turn from classical literature to Sacred Scripture. "The trajectory enacted by Jerome and described by Symon Wynter is exactly that followed by many of his Syon colleagues and successors," writes Vincent Gillespie.[86] Illustrating the importance of Jerome for the monks at Syon, Gillespie points to Thomas Betson's book, *A Right Profitable Treatyse* (printed by Wynkyn de Worde in 1500), which pictures Jerome on the frontispiece and includes many translated passages from Jerome's writings.

---

[84] Brantley provides a complete listing of the manuscript's 101 contents in *Reading in the Wilderness*, 307–25.

[85] See Vincent Gillespie, "Syon and the New Learning," in *The Religious Orders*, 75–95.

[86] Ibid., 77.

According to James Clark, the monks of Syon and Sheen produced "devotional and pastoral manuals" that, thanks to the age of print, "enjoyed the widest readership in the century before 1540" and "did [the] most to shape the piety of the literate laity."[87] In 1519, Wynkyn de Worde published *The Orchard of Syon*, a translation of Catherine of Siena's *Dialogues*.[88] At Syon Monastery, Richard Whitford (1495-1555?) edited the *Pomander of Prayer*, composed by an unnamed Carthusian at Sheen—a popular work that was printed and twice reprinted in London (1530-1532). Whitford himself authored *The Myrrour of Our Lady*, published in 1530, and the *Work for Householders*, printed by Wynkyn de Worde in 1530, reprinted in 1537 by John Wayland, and in 1538 by Robert Redman. The *Following of Christ*, Whitford's translation of the first three books of the *Imitation of Christ*, was published 1556, with a second edition appearing in 1585. Richard Pynson published Syon monk William Bond's *Pylgrimage of Perfection* in 1526.[89] Thomas Betson's *A Right Profitable Treatyse* addressed an audience of both lay and religious, providing translated excerpts from the Fathers of the Church alongside "basic [catechetical] instruction to the poorest of readers."[90]

---

[87] James G. Clark, "The Religious Orders in Pre-Reformation England," in *Religious Orders in Pre-Reformation England*, 3–33, at 19.

[88] See Sister Mary Denise, "*The Orchard of Syon*: An Introduction," *Traditio* 14 (1958): 269–93.

[89] Mary C. Erler, *Women, Reading, and Piety in Late Medieval England* (Cambridge: Cambridge University Press, 2002), 142.

[90] Alexandra Da Costa, *Marketing English Books, 1476–1550: How Printers Changed Reading* (Oxford: Oxford University Press, 2022), 37.

Conclusion

Unlike the figures we have surveyed here, most of the monks and nuns of late medieval England have left no extant, written record of their meditations, thoughts, and feelings. Long ago, Knowles lamented, "Of the spiritual life of the older orders and friars, indeed, we know next to nothing in this [fifteenth] century."[91] Over the past seventy-five years both church historians and literary scholars alike have done much to try to fill this gap.

Clearly the monasteries were straining to remain faithful to their spiritual and material inheritance and obligations in changed times: the older orders upheld *stabilitas loci* in part through promoting physical pilgrimage to the shrines of venerated saints and extending hospitality to strangers and neighbors alike; the younger orders (Carthusian, Bridgettine), zealously protected their own enclosure while teaching spiritual paths of pilgrimage. These younger orders called the older ones to stricter ascetical observance, while the older ones defended the value of moderation, flexibility, and abbatial discretion.

Despite manifold differences, both monastic streams emphasized the educational and formative mission of the monasteries for the laity through vernacular, devotional, and catechetical writings that reached the laity, but also circled back, in turn, to readers in the monasteries,

---

[91] Knowles, *Religious Orders*, 2:219.

instructing the instructors and creating a broader sense of community. Acceding to the wishes and accepting the commissions of the literate laity, the older and younger monasteries often shared the same benefactors, whom they also frequently admitted to confraternity. These included the devout nobility but also, increasingly, the members of wealthy merchant families.

I have avoided the topic of the Dissolution of the 1530s in these lectures. It is clear enough to all fair-minded historians nowadays that, while monastic reform was needed and was in fact ongoing, nothing in the preceding decades necessitated the Dissolution in the particular form in which it occurred. What is also clear, looking back, is that the Dissolution did not actually end monasticism in England. It continued in the sixteenth century and continues now, because the origins of monasticism are in the Sacred Scriptures themselves.

The Offices In Anglicanism Then And Now

Rev. Dr. Bryan D. Spinks

The Elizabethan Settlement

WITH THE ACCESSION of Queen Mary, the Protestant experiment in the Church of England came to an end. The Catholic Latin services came back into use and were welcomed in many circles. Mary reunited the English Church with Rome. However, she could not reverse the dissolution of the monasteries. Apart from establishing a Benedictine community at Westminster Abbey, the Henrician dissolution remained a *fait accompli*. With Mary's death in 1558 and the succession of her half-sister, Elizabeth, the Marian restoration was reversed, and after a short period of uncertainty, a new Act of Uniformity provided a slightly revised 1552 *Book of Common Prayer* as the lawful liturgy for the Church of England. Although there were some minor though not insignificant changes from 1552, the Offices of Morning and Evening Prayer remained unchanged. However, the Elizabethan Settlement was more complex and full of ambiguity.

The provision was made for regular public worship, and comprised the Litany and Suffrages, the *Book of Common Prayer (1559)*, and the Latin versions for the collegiate chapels of Oxford, Cambridge, Eton, and Winchester of 1560 and the corrected editions of 1571/2. There were also forms for occasional use, such as for days of fasting.[1] But a third category was the official primers and collections of prayers for private use which were issued at various dates from 1559 to 1590. This third category consisted of several distinct collections of devotional material. According to William Clay, these private devotional forms, set forth by authority (though the nature of the authority is debatable), fall into four groups.[2] The first is the primer, published in 1559, and another version in 1566, and a second edition in 1575. These are quite distinct from the reprints in 1560 and 1568 of the Edwardian primer (1553). Second is the *Orarium*, or Hours, in Latin, published in 1560 and 1573. Third is the Latin *Preces Privatae* of 1564, 1568, 1573 and 1574; and last, and very different from the primers, *The Book of Christian Prayers*, 1569,1578, 1581 and 1590. The 1559 primer, "set furth at large, with many godly and devoute Prayers," was published by John Wayland, *Cum privilegio ad imprimendum solum*. Indeed, the imprint declared,

---

[1]   Natalie Mears, Alastair Raffe, Stephen Taylor and Philip Williamson (with Lucy Bates), eds., *National Prayers: Special Worship Since the Reformation, Vol.1.: Special Prayers, Fasts and Thanksgivings in the British Isles 1533-1688* (Woodbridge, UK: The Church of England Record Office and the Boydell Press, 2013).

[2]   William K. Clay, ed., *Private Prayers Put forth by Authority during the Reign of Queen Elizabeth* (Cambridge: Cambridge University Press, 1851).

"forbyddyng all other to print this or any other Prymer."[3]
Ian Green points out that although Wayland still held the
monopoly, the title page confirms that it was published by
William Seres for the assigns of John Wayland. Seres had
permission to publish primers in Edward's reign, but he was
imprisoned during Mary's reign. Green surmises that Seres
may have done a deal with Wayland, and the "privilegium"
was Seres warning off Wayland and others not to trespass
on his preserves.[4] It was the 1551 version of Henry's 1545
primer. However, unlike that of 1551, it included the Preface
from the 1545 book–almost a reminder that the Church of
Elizabeth was but a continuation of the Henrician Church.
The preface reminded all and sundry that "IT IS the parte
of kynges (whom the Lorde hath constituted & sette for
pastours of his people" to procure not only a peaceable
life, but also provide for the true worship of God. Whereas
the 1559 *Book of Common Prayer* provided the two offices
of Morning and Evening Prayer, this book provided for
the eight offices in English, including office hymns. It
included the Seven Penitential Psalms, the 1544 Litany
(minus the petition against the bishop of Rome), *Dirige*
and Commendations, Psalms of the Passion, the reading
of the Passion, and a collection of prayers for a variety
of subjects unchanged from 1545. Of course, this primer
intended to replace Mary's primers, but it was certainly *not*

---

[3] Clay, *Private Prayers*, 2.

[4] Letter to the author April 27, 2009. My thanks to Dr. Ian Green for the
information about the printing of these primers and other devotional books, and for other very helpful observations.

the Edwardian primer of 1553, and makes provision for the traditional Catholic devotions, though without those addressed to the Virgin Mary, the saints, and angels. A further edition was issued in 1566, though here the Prayer Book catechism was included, and the Commendations were replaced by the fifteen penitential psalms which originated with Bishop John Fisher, and they were found in the Latin *Preces Privatae*. Whether by indirect Royal authority, or the choice of Seres, it is a reformed Henrician primer.

In 1560 the *Orarium* was published. This was a Latin primer. Its calendar is an extensive calendar of saints' days. It included the catechism, the eight hours, but compared to the English primer, it lacked the *Dirige* and the Commendations. In some ways this can be seen as an instructional primer and devotional in the language of university learning. Yet exactly what message was being sent about saints' days and about Latin hymns? This was to be republished in 1573. The first edition of the *Preces Privatae* appeared in 1564. It resembles the *Orarium*, but provides only for Morning and Evening Prayer, not the traditional eight hours, but retained antiphons and office hymns. The forms are not those of Morning and Evening Prayer of the *Book of Common Prayer* (1559). This collection included prayers and psalms for certain festivals, and a great variety of prayers, as well as prayers for grace at meals.

If the text of the *Book of Common Prayer* is a return to 1552, these other provisions hark back to the period

1545–1551. They encouraged a more traditional Catholic piety than that contained in the rites for public worship. An ambiguous Church settlement indeed. Yet, as these primers appeared in final editions in the 1570s, so *Christian Prayers and Meditations* was published in 1569 and with modifications and under the title *A Booke of Christian Prayers* in 1578 and would continue to appear in the 1590s. Elizabeth's Settlement restored the Cranmerian Offices for public worship but allowed the older hours, in modified form, in English and in Latin, for private use. We may assume that more conservative laity and clergy took advantage of this private use. Yet, by the late sixteenth century, recitation of the hours was beginning to fall out of favor even amongst Catholic laity. There was a huge demand for private prayers, not in primers and Books of Hours, and so as both catholic and protestant piety changed, so there was less demand for Books of Hours.

Music

As we shall see, the Elizabethan Church continued the musical traditions of Cathedrals, the Chapels Royal, and Collegiate Churches. However, in parish churches the rhythm of services quicky established itself as Communion three or four times a year, with the usual Sunday services being Morning Prayer, Litany, and Ante-communion with Sermon (the only place that mandated a sermon) and

Evening Prayer with Catechism. In many churches the only singing was the metrical psalmody of Thomas Sternhold and John Hopkins, and the services were mainly said. However, this meant that the Church of England was the sole Protestant church to base its main Sunday services on the Divine Office. Ulrich Zwingli (d. 1531), for example, developed a preaching service from the old medieval service of Prone, and for a while retained the Ave Maria from the old service. John Calvin's (d. 1564) rite was based on the final revisions at Strasbourg which were the Ante-communion. It also became the custom for clergy family to hold daily services in the vicarage, using some of the many devotional forms that publishers provided, and very few would have recited the Daily Office in Church. For most parish clergy, the offices were Sunday services only.

But the Chapels Royal, the Cathedrals, and Collegiate Churches were different. They had statutes, and that required the canons to say or sing the Office daily. It was the cathedrals that had mostly retained organs and a master of the music. The Henrician and later Protestant reforms provided for minor canons and lay vicars choral, as well as choir schools. Nicholas Orme says of Elizabeth:

> The injunctions of 1559 which her commissioners took round the country referred approvingly to the "laudable science of music" in church and ordered that it should be allowed to continue as long as it was "modest and distinct" so that the listeners could hear and understand the words that were being sung.[5]

---

[5] Nicholas Orme, *The History of England's Cathedrals* (Exeter, UK: Impress, 2017), 129.

And so, Thomas Tallis, William Byrd, and Orlando Gibbons were among the precursors of a long and distinguished line of composers who birthed the Anglican choral tradition of Matins and Evensong. In the Elizabethan Church it became a custom to sing a verse anthem after the Office, in imitation of an earlier tradition in medieval Vespers and Compline. It was not marked by a rubric until the 1662 *Book of Common Prayer*.

The Caroline Church and the Cromwellian Church

In the reign of Charles I (1625–1649), when the Durham House Group, or "Laudians," were in the ascendency, there was a move to recover some traditions lost at the Reformation. One example was perhaps prompted by the fact that Charles's Queen, a Catholic, had French ladies in waiting who used Catholic Books of Hours. John Cosin (d. 1672), a Prebendary of Durham, drew up a comparable book for the Protestant members of the Royal Household. In 1627 Cosin published *A Collection of Private Devotions* for the Anglican members of the Royal Court, which was attacked by more Puritan-minded clergy as a return to monastic prayer of popery.[6] Puritan suspicions were also aroused by the family and friends of

---

[6] P. G. Stanwood, ed., *John Cosin, A Collection of Private Devotions* (Oxford: Clarendon Press, 1967); Bryan D. Spinks, "What was wrong with Mr. Cosin's couzening Devotions? Deconstructing an Episode in Seventeenth-Century Anglican 'Liturgical Hagiography,'" *Worship* 74 (2000): 308–29.

Nicholas Ferrer (d. 1637) at Little Gidding. This extended community gathered daily for prayer at certain hours, in addition to Morning and Evening Prayer of the Prayer Book. Prayers began at 4:00 a.m. in summer and 5:00 a.m. in winter. These "Hours" consisted of psalms, a reading from a harmony on the Gospels and one of the hymns of George Wither, accompanied by a harmonium. In the ill-fated 1637 Scottish Prayer Book, often erroneously referred to as "Laud's liturgy," a new versicle and response were added to the opening versicles of Morning and Evening Prayer: "Praise ye the Lord. The Lord's name be praised."

The Durham House experiments and the Cathedral choral tradition were both interrupted and ended in the Interregnum after the English Civil War. The Church of England as an Episcopal Church was dismantled to be replaced by a semi-Presbyterian and Congregationalist tradition. The Cromwellian Church had no use for Cathedrals, and many were used for other purposes or simply closed. The use of the *Book of Common Prayer* was made illegal. In 1658 Jeremy Taylor (d. 1667) published *A Collection of Offices*, which gave services for Morning and Evening that were suggested by the *Book of Common Prayer* but had a different text and drew on the Greek Orthodox form of confession.[7] The layman, Owen Felltham published *A Form of Prayer for family use.*[8] The details of

---

[7] See the discussion Harry Boone Porter, *Jeremy Taylor: Liturgist* (London: SPCK 1979), 51–7.

[8] Ted Larry Pebworth, "An Anglican Family Worship Service of the Interregnum: A Cancelled Early Text and a New Edition of Owen Felltham's 'A Form of Prayer,'" *English Literary Renaissance* 16 (1986): 206–33.

all of these are not necessary to rehearse, but they all point to experimentation and the need for a regular rhythm but something different from the Prayer Book forms.

1662, the Non-Jurors, and the American Book

With the Restoration Settlement, a revised *Book of Common Prayer* of 1662 was enacted, and in England, it still remains not only an authorized liturgy, but the only one which is backed by an Act of Parliament. In 1662 the permissible use of an anthem was now marked by rubric. The choral tradition of the cathedrals was restored and continued to develop, though the standard differed amongst cathedrals, some being better than others.

The crisis of the flight of James II in 1689 and the invitation to William of Orange and his Stuart wife, Mary, sparked off the Non-Juring split—those clergy, including the Archbishop of Canterbury, who, having taken an oath to James and his successors, were unable in conscience to take an oath to William and Mary. Their ranks—never very large—were further swelled by further secessions with the House of Hanover. Anglicans, particularly in the twentieth century, have been captivated by the liturgical experiments of the Non-Jurors, particularly their use of Apostolic Constitutions, and the liturgy of St. James for Eucharistic liturgies. Worth remembering is that Non-Juring congregations were very small, so these liturgies were never widely used. Often overlooked is the 1734 *A Compleat Collection of Devotions*, by Bishop Thomas Deacon (d. 1753), Non-Juring Bishop of Manchester, which contained daily private prayers for morning and evening, and for nine, twelve, and three o'clock. In trawling through the older liturgical traditions, Deacon was inspired to find devotions to mark these hours. Once again, it must be stressed that these forms were probably available to and used by very few people.

In America, the need for a separate church from that of England led to the Protestant Episcopal Church of the United States, and the 1789/90 Book of Common Prayer was adopted rather than the Philadelphia Book of 1786. This latter had omitted the words "priest" and "absolution," but 1789 restored most of the references to priest. At Evening Prayer, the *Magnificat* and *Nunc Dimittis* were both removed, thus weakening the historic link with Vespers and Compline.

The Tractarian Revival

Much more important for the developing global Anglican church was the influence of the Tractarian movement, Nashotah House being one of its legacies. The first Tractarians urged that all clergy should observe the rubrics of the *Book of Common Prayer*, which would include daily recitation of the Offices as in cathedrals.

In Tract 9 of *The Tracts for the Times* Hurrel Froude (d. 1836) addressed those who wanted the services shortened. Froude argued that they had already been shortened at the Reformation and had been intended to be used daily. They had become weekly, and if the trend continued, they would become monthly, and then disappear. The Oxford scholars began to look back at pre-Reformation usages and services and in England appealed to the ornaments rubric and the Elizabethan injunctions to restore ceremonial. John Henry Newman (d. 1890) had begun using the Roman Breviary in 1837, and Edward Pusey (d. 1882) did the same in 1839. Second-generation Tractarians, and the more advanced Anglo-Papalists, used the Roman forms, certainly during the week. But the use of the Breviary became accelerated by the re-founding of religious communities in the Church of England. Monasteries and convents needed more than the Prayer Book forms of Morning and Evening Prayer, so either contemporary Roman, or pre-Reformation English Uses were adapted and adopted. This was a reminder that the Prayer Book Offices, though derived from the "Monastic" office, and though themselves heavily monastic in form, were never intended for the devotional needs of communities of Religious, since by the time they were compiled, there were no longer any religious communities. Anglican Religious continue to use Hours, comparable to the Roman Catholic Daily Office, as do some Parish clergy. The Cistercian Community at Ewell held Vigils at 4:00 a.m., prayer and reading at 7:30 a.m., Eucharist and Terce after

Breakfast, Sext at noon, None at 3:00 p.m., Vespers at 5:45
p.m., and Compline at 7:30 p.m.[9]

However, the ripples of the Tractarians did spill over
into many Anglican provinces, and many agreed with the
1906 Royal Commission pronouncement in England that
the then-current liturgical provisions were too narrow
for the religious life of Anglicans. In 1914 the Episcopal
Church USA published *A Book of Offices* which contained
an order for Compline, which seemed to have become
increasingly popular. Several revisions of prayer books took
place around 1927–1929, and in both the American 1928
book and the proposed book for England 1927 and 1928,
Compline was included.

And Now

Only in the wake of the liturgical revisions of the
Roman Catholic Church and the implications of the tenets
of the Liturgical Movement did attention begin to be paid
to the Divine Office at an official provincial level. The
proposed reforms of the 1970s and 1980s were conservative
in nature. One reason was that all the revisers' energies
were poured into eucharistic and baptismal liturgies, and
many studies that were available were not translated into
English. The implications of the work by scholars such as

[9] Aelred Arnesen, *The Possibilities of Prayer in the 21st Century: The
Anglican Cistercians of Ewell Monastery - Essays on Worship* (Victoria, CA:
Trafford Publishing, 2007), 76.

Paul Bradshaw and Robert Taft were only beginning to be absorbed by liturgical scholars and then a trickle down to those concerned with revision. The Offices in the 1979 *Book of Common Prayer* are a good example of the partial absorption of the newer insights. It provides excellent forms for Noonday and Evening which are short, succinct, and accessible to laity with busy lives. The forms for Morning and Evening Prayer, though, are Cranmer-enriched and not revised. In my opinion they are cumbersome, turgid, and still heavily monastic in their content. Andrew McGowan, in his consideration of the Divine Office of 1979 Prayer Book, wrote:

> The main offices of Morning and Evening Prayer are in fact among the most conservative elements of the book, and reflect little either of fresh contemporary insight, or of that wisdom older even than Cranmer's and derived from ancient Christian patterns of worship, on which those who formed the 1979 book drew in many other ways.[10]

This was also true of the Church of England's *Alternative Service Book* 1980. The Offices were Cranmer-enriched and turned into modern journalese, and revisers then wondered why cathedrals would not trade the 1662 forms with their musical repertoire for these new music-less forms.

Again, by the insights of modern liturgical scholarship, these too were monastic forms. Such forms can be maintained in a seminary setting where we still extract

[10] Andrew McGowan, "Moving Offices: Daily Prayer in the 1979 Book of common Prayer and Beyond," in *Issues in Prayer Book Revision,* ed. Robert W. Pritchard (New York: Church Publishing Incorporated, 2018), 49-70, at 50.

ordinands from the normal life of the Church and make them into a temporary religious community. However, the moral pressure and a fundamentalist approach to the canons are then brought to bear on clergy to recite these Offices Daily in their parish life which is to impose a monastic Office on secular clergy and can become a lonely burden.[11] It is conveniently forgotten that the "Cathedral" Office was congregational, and not for solitary recitation; it was cantillated or sung, not said.

A New Zealand Prayer Book of 1989 has become quite popular, especially among Episcopal Clergy. Its daily Services are short, succinct, and user-friendly.

In *Common Worship* 2000, the Church of England, by accident, broke the mold. Like Cranmer, they were inspired by Franciscans. The Liturgical Commission was approached by the Anglican Society of St. Francis who were about to revise their office book, and they wished to know what the Commission had in mind so that the Franciscans were not out of step with the rest of the Church of England. The result was that some members of the Society, some members of the Commission, and one or two others who had floated ideas or published private office books worked as a sub-contracted group. The result was *Celebrating Common Prayer,* which was published in a Franciscan edition and a wider church edition. This incorporated a more "Cathedral" style with hymns and psalmody

---

[11] *Guidelines for the Professional Conduct of the Clergy,* (Church of England), Revised edition (London: Church House Publishing, 2015), 10–11.

appropriate to the time of day, and shorter readings, as well as psalm collects, short intercessions, and seasonal material. The book was commended by the archbishops and became the foundation of *Common Worship Daily Prayer*. It has not dislodged the 1662 choral versions in cathedrals but is significantly different to attract new musical composition. The forms are not simply 1662 in modern English. Morning Prayer for Sunday and daily in Eastertide begins with only one versicle and response, followed by a "Berakah"-style blessing of God. Week I and Sundays in Easter then have Psalm 100 and the Psalms all end with a Psalm Collect. A canticle follows from a choice of four, and then a short Scripture reading, according to the week and day. A versicle and response introduce the *Benedictus,* which is followed by short intercessions, a Collect, and optional Lord's Prayer. The Office ends with the versicle and response, "Let us Bless the Lord, Thanks be to God." There is an expanded edition for the Franciscan Order, acknowledging the different needs for different groups.

These broad brushstrokes of some trends from 1559 up to today provide some framework for remarks about the spiritual and devotional value of the Office in Anglicanism. In many parts of the Anglican Communion, the success of the Liturgical Movement and the Parish Communion movement have resulted in the Eucharist replacing Morning Prayer as the main service; and with the decline in church attendance, Sunday Choral Evensong is either monthly or has ceased. Cranmer's planned Franciscan reform of the Benedictine reform has ceased to work. The familiarity with the whole psalter, canticles, and the breadth of Scripture has seeped away. And yet, in choral foundations, Daily and Sunday Evensong is alive and well and serves as an example of a monastic office that seems to work well for congregational attendance. Timothy Day has pointed out that there does exist an English Anglican myth that this choral tradition reaches back to the sixteenth century, but, in fact, it derives from the late nineteenth century when there was considerable internal reform of the English Cathedrals.[12] Attendance is the operative word, since the congregation's participation is limited to silent following of the psalms and canticles and the inclusion of a hymn. Yet if that was not what Cranmer may have envisaged as participation, it is still a popular means of spiritual participation. In his recent part-historic and part-devotional reflection on Choral Evensong, Simon Reynolds sees an interest in pilgrimage of various types and monastic way of prayer as part of present culture, of which the continued popularity of Choral Evensong is part. He writes,

> Not only did Evensong evolve from the monastic pattern of daily prayer, it continues to offer a stable, reliable and regular pattern of daily worship. In one sense, it makes few demands because it is simply given. It usually happens at a time when people are heading home from work, or have finished school or shopping, visiting people in hospital, a

---

[12] Timothy Day, *I Saw Eternity the Other Night. King's College Choir, the Nine Lessons and Carols, and an English Singing Style* (London: Penguin, Random House, 2018). The reforms were probably in part spurred on by John Jebb's 1843 account of the poor music in many of the Cathedrals.

care home or prison, when the axis of the day begins to turn from light to darkness, It offers a space into which the concerns, failures and achievements of the day can be brought into the wide and generous orbit if the Church's worship . . . Choral Evensong is worship that respects the integrity and uniqueness of each person, without ever coercing us to reinvent ourselves or adopt a new identity.[13]

Reynolds notes how the custom is to add intercessions after the choir anthem, and this is a place where members of the congregation can inwardly insert their own concerns, doubts, fears, and joys. This tradition took its present shape in the nineteenth century with the voluntary reform of cathedrals and collegiate foundations, and they are places to showcase the choral history of the Anglican Office, but also a site that attracts new compositions.

But what are we to make of the more recent revisions which depart from Cranmer? There is a recognition that what might have been envisaged for the Church and society in the sixteenth century does not generally provide for Anglicans now. The new forms are concerned to mark times of the day with appropriate but limit psalmody, a fixed canticle alongside a variety of choices, short intercessions, and a limited amount of Scripture to inspire meditation rather than extended instruction. Meditative rather than instructional might sum it all up. Such new Offices still draw on the monastic tradition but attempt to create not so much a monastic office, or a clergy office, but a meditative office

[13] Simon Reynolds, *Lighten our Darkness. Discovering and Celebrating Choral Evensong* (London: Darton, Longman and Todd, 2021), 20 and 26.

for spiritual people who live, move, and have their being in a busy and hectic secular world. Use of selected psalmody and prayer for each particular time of day recaptures something of what contemporary scholars believe was at the center of the old ancient "Cathedral" Office and provides a rich devotional fare for spiritual sustenance.